The Dominant Strain

(Anna Chapin Ray)

CHAPTER ONE

Beatrix smiled a little wearily. Intimate friends are sometimes cloying, and she felt a certain irritation rising within her, as she watched Sally's bright face under her French toque, and listened to the easy stream of chatter which issued from Sally's lips. Sally had never faced such a crisis as the one confronting Beatrix, that day. Moreover, she had dimples, and it was impossible to believe in the sympathy of a person whose dimples insisted upon coming into sight, even in the midst of serious discussion.

"If he hasn't already," Sally persisted; "he is bound to do it before the season is over. Then what shall you tell him?"

"Aren't you rushing things a little?" Beatrix inquired languidly. "Please do remember that I only met Mr. Lorimer at the Horse Show, and that it is three weeks to Lent."

"That's nothing," Sally replied flatly, but flippantly. "You subjugated Eric Stanford in half that time, and his gray matter has been in a pulpy condition ever since."

"I didn't know it."

"About his gray matter?"

"Oh, that is congenital trouble. I mean I didn't know that I had subjugated him. Besides, that is different. He was Bobby Dane's chum, and we took him into the family."

"Took him in all over," Sally drawled.

Beatrix's eyes flashed. There were things she would not say to Sally; there were also things which Sally could not say to her.

"I am so sorry," she said, as she rose; "but I must get ready for Mrs. Stanley's recital. How does it happen you aren't going?"

"For the most ignominious of reasons. I'm not bidden. Mrs. Stanley and I were on a committee together, once upon a time. We squabbled over some amateur theatricals, and she has cut my acquaintance ever since. I always did say that there is nothing like amateur theatricals for bringing out all the worst vices of humanity. If a Shakespearian revival ever reaches the heavenly host, Gabriel and Michael will have to play Othello and Iago turn and turn about, to prevent ill-feeling. Beatrix?"

"Well?"

"What do you honestly think of Mr. Lorimer?"

Beatrix hesitated. Then she faced her friend.

"That he is the most interesting man we have met, this season."

"That's not saying any too much. Still, it is an admission. Are you going to marry him?"

"He hasn't asked me."

"But he will."

"How do you know?"

"I do know."

"I'm not so sure of it." Beatrix laughed nervously.

"But if he does?"

"I--I'm not so sure of that, either."

"Beatrix! Why not?"

Beatrix untied the long ribbons which belted her gown, and stood drawing them slowly through and through her fingers. Sally leaned back in her deep chair and watched her friend keenly, mercilessly. She and Beatrix had fenced long enough; it was time for the direct thrust. Sidney Lorimer was the most available man on that winter's carpet. Moreover, for weeks he had been a patient follower in the wake of Beatrix Dane. Beatrix might be as impenetrable as she chose; but Sally knew that, during the past week, she had been reading the headings of certain suppressed chapters in Lorimer's history, and that they had changed her whole attitude towards the man. The signs were slight, too slight for him to have recognized them as yet; but Sally's curious, pitiless eyes had discerned them. She had discerned and disapproved, and she had resolved that no squeamish delicacy should keep her from preventing Beatrix's playing the part of a prude.

"He is the best-looking man of the season, and the best dancer. He took honors at Göttingen. He has any quantity of money." Sally ticked off the points on the tips of her gray glove. "And most of all," she tapped her thumb conclusively, "he is very much in love with Miss Beatrix Dane, and I want him to marry her."

"Oh, Sally, do be sensible!" Beatrix burst out impatiently. Then she pulled herself up sharply and turned to bay. "What about the Forbes supper?" she demanded.

Sally shrugged her shoulders, as she fastened her fur collar.

"Oh, Beatrix, you prig! Are there any men of our set who haven't been a little frisky?"

"Frisky! That is a milder word than I should use, Sally. The Forbes affair transcends friskiness and becomes the beginning of the pace that kills. It was intolerable; I can't forgive it."

Her face flushed; then it paled and hardened with the rigidity of self-control. Sally peered out at her through lowered lashes, and judged that it was time for her to remove herself. She had known Beatrix from their childhood, and this was the first time she had seen her jarred from her self-possession. She fastened the last hook with a jerk. Then she rose and went to her friend's side.

"I didn't mean to tease you, dear," she said penitently. "I know this has been worrying you; but don't let it get on your nerves and influence you too much. All men make slips at times. Mr. Lorimer is a good fellow, even if he has been a little fast. He would drop all that as soon as he was--settled. Besides, this isn't nearly as bad as ever so many of the stories we hear."

"No," Beatrix assented drearily; "but it is bad enough."

"Then you do care?"

"Care!" She laughed a little harshly. "Sally, truly I must send you off. It is time I was dressing, for I promised to go. I am sorry, but--"

"I am used to being dismissed; I shall come again." There was no hint of rancor in Sally's tone, yet she went away fully convinced that her own system of measurement could never reach the heights and the depths of her friend's mood.

Left to herself, Beatrix forgot her need for haste. She dropped down into a chair, and sat for many moments brooding over the fire. Her hand shielded her face; yet it could not conceal the anxious lines above her eyes nor the drooping lips. Lorimer had asked permission to call upon her, that evening, and she knew by instinct what the evening was holding in store for her. Confronted with the final decision, she was at a loss which course to take. Should she close her eyes to the plague-spot which might one day spread and spread until it tainted her whole life? The present was very tempting. Why not take it, and ignore the future? Most girls would wink at the suspicion which, during the past week, had been clouding her dream of perfect content. How far was she accountable for the future?

She dressed hurriedly; but when she reached Mrs. Stanley's house, the recital had already begun, and she dropped into a seat outside the music-room door. The artist was a new star upon the horizon. She had supposed him to be only one of the vast milky way which helped to shed a dim light upon Mrs. Stanley, as that good lady clambered slowly up the social ladder. Instead of that, Beatrix entirely forgot Mrs. Stanley's antics, in watching for the star itself. She even dismissed Lorimer from her mind, as she bent forward in eager listening to the invisible singer.

"Great fellow, Schubert!" her cousin observed, sauntering up to her side as soon as the recital was ended. "They say that this Thayer is daft upon the subject of him. Anyway, he manages to interpret him fairly well. What did you think?"

She pulled herself out of her absorption and laughed.

"Don't expect me to analyze him, Bobby. He is past that."

"Bad or good?"

"Good, if making havoc of my nerve centres is any test."

"Then you really liked him? I thought you didn't want to come."

"I didn't. Nothing but a stern sense of duty brought me; but it also brought its own reward. One hears such a voice only once a decade."

Bobby Dane eyed her askance.

"Sure this is yourself, Beatrix? I thought you scoffed at all baritones, and only delighted in maudlin tenors and anticking sopranos. I have hopes of you yet; but whence comes your conversion?"

"From this man, Mr. ----." She referred to the programme in her hand.

"Thayer," her cousin prompted. "Cotton Mather Thayer."

Beatrix gasped.

"Bobby! What a name for an artist!"

"For a punster, you'd better say; but at least one can't doubt its genuineness. If he had been going to assume a stage name, he would have chosen something more romantic."

"Who is he, and where did Mrs. Stanley accumulate him?"

Bobby rolled his eyes expressively towards the portly, satin-clad figure of his hostess.

"Mrs. Stanley hunts every lion that comes to Manhattan Island. As a rule, she catches only cubs; this is the exception which proves the rule."

"I haven't heard the name before."

"No; Thayer is a brand-new lion, but fully grown. Of course, with that name, his family tree sprouted in Massachusetts; but he has been in Germany and Italy for years. He only landed, the third, and is to make his formal début at the Lloyd Avalons's on the twentieth. Don't you want to meet him?"

"N--no. I am afraid it would be anticlimax."

"Not a bit of it. He doesn't indulge in speckled neckties and an imperial. He is a man, as well as a singer."

"You know him, then?"

"Yes, as one knows any number of people. Lorimer has had him at the club occasionally, and I have met him there."

"Mr. Lorimer?"

"Lorimer knew him well in Germany. Come and help burn incense before him, and do try to say something rational. Those fellows must get deadly sick of the inanities people talk when they are being introduced. If you make a good impression, perhaps I'll bring him around, some Monday."

"Wait till you see what impression he makes, Bobby. I'm not Mrs. Stanley, you know, and I'm not stalking any lions."

Even while he laughed at the sudden hauteur of her tone, he allowed his glance to wander over her with manifest approval.

"Good for you, Beatrix! But Thayer is a gentleman first of all, then an artist. A cad always shows himself at a strange club; but Thayer passed muster at The Critic, where even Lorimer isn't altogether popular."

"Why not?" she demanded sharply.

"Difference in taste in jokes," her cousin replied evasively. "I only spoke of it to show you that you were safe enough in knowing Thayer. Lorimer is a good fellow; even good fellows have their foes."

"But if Mr. Thayer hasn't--"

"Thayer hasn't been here long enough to get them. Give him time, Beatrix. Inside of six weeks, he will have every singer in New York slandering him. There's nothing more lovable than the way musicians stand by one another, when it's a case of fighting a successful rival."

She laughed suddenly.

"How do you know, Bobby? You're not a musician."

"Heaven forfend! If I were, I should spend half my time on The Island, doing sentence for battery and breach of the peace. I have known a few musicians in my time, Beatrix, and I know their pleasant little ways."

They had joined the large group gathered at the head of the music-room, and were slowly working their way from the outer fringe to the focal point. As they waited, now advancing a step, then halting again, Beatrix listened in some scorn to the fugue of praise which rose about her, a fugue composed chiefly of adjectives heaped in confusion about the single, magical noun *temperament*. She shot a mischievous glance up at her tall cousin.

"Fancy any man having to live up to this sort of thing, Bobby! *Divine* and *perfectly elegant* do not suggest the same set of attributes, and I don't see how he can strike the golden mean between them. Somebody really ought to coin a new word for such emergencies as this."

Before her cousin could answer, the woman just ahead of them had buried the singer's hand in her own pudgy clasp.

"Oh, Mr. Thayer, that was such a pretty piece you sang last! It was a German piece; wasn't it? It was just sweet!"

And it was after such a prelude that Beatrix bowed in recognition of her cousin's introduction. Even as she bowed, there came a swift realization that she was facing no anticlimax. And yet the man before her was in no wise the typical musician. Tall, so tall that Bobby Dane, five feet ten in his stockings, seemed short beside him, well-dressed, well-groomed, he looked far more like a prosperous, alert man of affairs than an artist or a dreamer. Moreover, in spite of certain lines in his face, he was absurdly boyish to have sung those great songs. He could know nothing of the real issues of fate with which he had been juggling, could have no real conception of either hope or disappointment. Doubtless he had developed his *Weltschmerz* mechanically, imitatively, at so many marks or *lire* an hour.

Beatrix had always been distressed by the flatness of her one-syllabled name. It gained a new roundness now; and she raised her eyes, as Thayer spoke it, to meet the gray ones above her. They were clear and steady eyes, smiling, yet with a look in their depths which to her mind accounted for the insistent, troubled note in his singing. The lines about his shaven lips were firm, but mobile.

Bobby eyed the two of them quizzically. Then he broke in upon the tentative conversation which follows an introduction.

"Pass, Beatrix! That's quite original. I told my cousin, Thayer, that if she could hail you with a new adjective, I should present you as a candidate for a dish of tea, some Monday."

As usually happened with Bobby Dane's remarks, this proved the end of any serious talk, and Beatrix laughed, as she responded,--

"Please come alone, Mr. Thayer. My cousin monopolizes all the conversation, when he is present."

"And Miss Dane always demands a good listener. Like a conspirator, she relies upon your silence, Thayer."

"What a restful hostess!" Thayer answered lightly. Then, turning, he laid a kindly hand on the arm of his accompanist. "Otto, I wish you to meet Mr. Dane. Miss Dane, may I introduce my friend, Mr. Arlt?"

It was done simply; but the boy blushed with sudden shyness before the stately girl, whose fur collar alone had cost far more than his whole year's expenses. Beatrix met him cordially, for she had seen him standing ignored in his corner by the piano, and she liked the friendly way in which the singer had included him in the trivial talk. It was not until afterwards that she suddenly recalled the fact that she herself and her cousin were apparently the only ones to whom Thayer had introduced his companion. She pondered over the reason for this until, as she slowly mounted the steps to her own door, she abruptly recurred to the unanswered question which had been driven from her mind by the afternoon's events.

The old butler met her in the hall.

"Mr. Lorimer has just telephoned to you, Miss Beatrix. He can't come, to-night, he says. His horse stumbled and threw him just now, and his ankle is sprained. It will be a few days before he can go out."

And with utter thankfulness Beatrix accepted even this brief reprieve.

CHAPTER TWO

"Cast your bread upon the waters, and it will come floating back to you in time to be fed out to the next man."

"Bad for the next man's digestion, though!" Bobby Dane commented, as he set down his empty cup. "You needn't offer me any of your second-hand pabulum, Beatrix."

"You probably will be in such dire straits that I shall offer you the first chance at it, Bobby," she retorted.

"Another cup of tea, and two pieces of lemon, please," Sally demanded. "What is the particular appositeness of your remarks, Beatrix?"

"Mr. Arlt and Mrs. Stanley. Also the conservation of philanthropic energy."

Sally stirred her tea with a protesting clatter of the spoon.

"Beatrix, I am glad I didn't go to college. Your mind is appalling; your language is more so. May I ask whether you are going into slumming?"

"No. Worse."

"For the family credit, I must draw the line at the Salvation Army," Bobby adjured her. "A poke bonnet and a tambourine wouldn't be a proper fruitage for our family tree."

"What are you going to do, Beatrix?" Sally repeated. "It is something uncanny, I know. I felt it in the air, and that was the reason I stayed until everybody else had gone. I knew you wished to confess."

"But I didn't."

"Not even to ease your conscience?"

"My conscience is perfectly easy."

"But you said it was worse than slumming."

"It is. Slumming is aristocratic and conservative; I am about to be radical."

"Don't tell me it is spectacles and statistics," Bobby pleaded. "I abhor statistical women; they are so absorbed in collating material that they never listen to the point of even your best stories."

"Not a statistic, I promise you, Bobby."

"Nor a poke bonnet?"

"No; my choice is for toques, not pokes. Do you know Mr. Arlt?"

"Never heard of the gentleman." Bobby's tone expressed cheery indifference, as he bent over to prod the fire.

"But you met him, Bobby."

"It was in a crowd, then, and it doesn't signify that I've heard of him. Who is he, Sally?"

With the freedom born of intimacy, Sally was eating up her lemon rind, and there was a momentary pause, while she shook her head. Beatrix answered the question.

"He is Mr. Thayer's accompanist, that little German who was with him at Mrs. Stanley's."

"Have you heard Thayer yet, Sally?" Bobby asked parenthetically.

"No. I have heard about him till I am weary of his name, though, and such a name! Cotton Mather Thayer!"

"Did it ever occur to you the handicap of going through life as Bobby?" inquired the owner of that name. "It is a handicap; but it is also a distinct advantage. Nobody ever expects me to amount to anything. No matter how much I fizzle, they'll say 'Oh, but it's only Bobby Dane!' Now, Cotton Mather Thayer is bound to fill a niche in the--the--"

"Lofty cathedral of fame reared by the ages." Sally helped him out of his rhetorical abyss.

"Thanks awfully; yes. And then Beatrix will scatter her water-soaked breadcrumbs around him to coax the little sparrows to make their nests in the crown of his hat and get free music lessons for their young in exchange for keeping his head warm."

Beatrix frowned; then she laughed. Bobby was incorrigible, and there was no use in expecting seriousness from him. He and Sally were alike; Beatrix was cast in a different mould. She could suffer and enjoy with an intensity unknown to either of the others; yet she was close kin to her cousin in her appreciation of his irresponsible fun, even though it would never have occurred to her to originate it. Moreover, even if it had occurred to her, it is doubtful whether she could have accomplished it.

"Who gets first bite at your bread, Beatrix?" Bobby asked encouragingly. "Granted that Arlt, whoever he is, gets second nibble, who comes in ahead?"

"Mrs. Stanley." In spite of herself, Beatrix laughed at the logical application of her metaphor. Stout, energetic Mrs. Stanley was so like a greedy young turkey snapping up the crumbs dropped from the hands of her superiors.

Sally raised her brows.

"Knowing Mrs. Stanley's appetite, I only wonder that any of the loaves and fishes should be left over," she drawled maliciously.

"Mrs. Stanley has her good points, Sally."

Bobby interrupted.

"Not a point. She is all built in parabolic curves. Why can't you be accurate, Beatrix, as befits your higher education? You took conic sections a year before I did."

"All the more reason I should forget them sooner. Besides, haven't I begged you not to allude to the fact that I am a year older than you?"

"But is Mr. Thayer as great a singer as they say?" Sally asked, with sudden irrelevancy.

"Greater. He is almost perfectly satisfactory."

"Not quite?"

"Not yet; he will be, some day, if he can only have an unhappy love affair," Beatrix answered placidly, as she rose from the tea table and crossed to the open fire.

"That is an humane speech."

"Artistic, though. He needs just that to develop him. He strikes every note but tenderness."

"Tenderness is generally located at *C in Alt*, Beatrix. A baritone can't soar to that height; you should be content when he growls defiance and moans resignation."

"Besides," Sally suggested; "it is quite within the limits of possibility that Mr. Thayer might have a happy love affair. Would that answer your purpose, Beatrix?"

"Not in the least. It is his minor key that needs developing."

"Never mind," Bobby added. "Artists are scheduled for the unhappy loves. Therein lies the advantage of being merely a newspaper man."

Sally looked up inquiringly.

"Just what is it that you do, Bobby? I know you have a desk and a salary; but I've never been able to find out that you did anything but put your heels on one and your fingers on the other."

"That's because you aren't there to see."

"No; but I have heard. Do you ever work, really work?"

"Of course I work. I earn the jam to eat on my daily bread. I boxed the devil's ears, this morning."

"Luther *redivivus*! You and Beatrix will soon be great moral forces in the metropolis. Beatrix, is he really presentable?"

"Bobby, or the devil?"

"Neither. Mr. Th--"

"Mr. Thayer," the old butler announced imperturbably, and the subject of discussion came slowly across the great dusky room towards the circle of light around the table.

Even while she was suppressing her gasp of sheer embarrassment, Sally admitted to herself that he was presentable, very presentable. His manner was altogether free from the self-conscious graciousness of an artist off-duty; moreover, he was very big, very comely, very much stamped with the hall-mark of her own class. His eyes were steady; his shoulders were broad, but his hands were slim. As for Sally Van Osdel, she had one attribute of a great general; she knew how to beat a dignified retreat from an awkward situation, and she it was who broke in upon the little pause which followed the introductions.

"Your entrance was most dramatic, Mr. Thayer, for your name was just trembling upon our lips. Miss Dane has been asking us if we knew your accompanist, Mr. Arlt."

He turned to Beatrix.

"Otto? What about him, Miss Dane?"

"Only good. Miss Gannion was speaking to me about him, last night."

"You know Miss Gannion?"

"Who doesn't?"

He laughed silently from between his close-shut teeth.

"That can be interpreted in two senses."

"Not if you know Miss Gannion. She is of the salt of the earth."

"I am glad to hear you say so. She is the one person in the city to whom I brought an introduction. She was out when I called, so I am still a good deal at sea in regard to her."

A direct question would have been unpardonable; but Beatrix could see no offence in the note of interrogation in his voice.

"She is a dear little spinster of fifty, with endless interests and not a hobby to her name, the most downright, practical person I have ever known, and the most helpful to strangers and pilgrims in the city. It is quite incidental that she is uncommonly rich and uncommonly homely. Nobody ever stops to think about either fact."

"And she has heard of Arlt?"

"Yes, she hears of everybody. She has a great talent for putting young men on their feet and teaching them to walk alone. In fact, she is a perfect employment bureau for meritorious youth. Somebody wrote to her that Mr. Arlt has genius and grit, and not a guinea to his name, and she is trying to get him some engagements."

"She asked you to help him?"

"Yes. At least, she spoke about him, and asked me to keep my eyes open and to say a good word for him, when I can. What does he want, Mr. Thayer?"

"Whatever he can get."

"What does he need, then?"

"Everything." Thayer's tone was grave.

"At least, that is comprehensive, Beatrix," her cousin assured her. "He may even be starved into eating your chloride of manna."

She ignored the interruption.

"And you have known him for some time, Mr. Thayer?"

"Long enough to have no hesitation in vouching for him, both as a man and as an artist." His tone was not unfriendly, yet it was of dignified finality.

"Then why the deuce hasn't the fellow arrived?" Bobby rose, as he spoke, and planted his feet accurately on the middle pothook of the hearthrug.

"Chiefly because art is long, and we are all too busy to wait for it to display itself. Give him time," Sally suggested idly, for she was becoming a little bored by the discussion.

"Time is money, though. Perhaps a pension would do just as well."

Thayer frowned involuntarily. To him, his art was too sacred to admit of any flippancy in discussing it. He turned still more directly to Beatrix.

"Arlt is a thoroughly good fellow, one you are safe in introducing anywhere. He is only a boy, barely twenty; but he is one of the most satisfactory pianists I have ever heard. I don't mean I haven't heard better ones; but never one who has been more satisfying to my mood, whatever it is. His technique is not perfect, and he lacks maturity; but he has a trick of making people dissatisfied with other pianists and anxious to hear him play the same programme."

"And he will accompany?"

"Ye-es. Sometimes."

Beatrix laughed.

"I spare your modesty, Mr. Thayer. I think I understand. But really I haven't much influence. If I can help him, though, you can count on my doing it."

"All he needs is a little start. As Miss Van Osdel says, New York is moving too fast to wait for strangers to fall into step with the procession."

"He is a stranger, then?"

"He came over with me." Thayer hesitated. "I may as well tell you a bit about him," he went on. "It can't do any harm, and it may supplement Miss Gannion's story. He is that unhappy being, the youngest son of a younger son, and he has more ancestors than money. His father ran away to escape army service, and forgot to provide for his wife and children. The children died, all but two, Otto and a sister eight years older. He was half through his musical training, when she had a fall that crippled her, and the boy had to give up study and take to teaching. For two years, he fought a losing fight, giving lessons to stolid youngsters, playing at cheap concerts wherever he could get an engagement, and all the time slowly dropping deeper and deeper into debt. One night, he fainted in the middle of the accompaniment to *The Erl-King*, and it looked as if the King had claimed him. There were a couple of Americans in the hall who had been watching him for weeks, and they began to investigate the case. Arlt, it seems, hadn't eaten anything for two days; and, just as he had started for the concert, he had received legal notice that the next day his mother and sister would be turned into the street, because the rent was unpaid."

"And then?" Sally queried, as Thayer came to a full stop.

"Then they took him out to supper," he replied prosaically.

"And then?" Sally persisted.

Thayer spoke with some reluctance.

"Then they found him an engagement that paid a better salary, and they bullied him into accepting a little loan, until the first week's payday came around."

"That was so good of you!" Beatrix said impulsively.

He raised his brows.

"I wasn't the only American in Berlin at the time, Miss Dane."

"No; you said there were two of you. But there is no use in your denying that you were the one who sang *The Erl-King*."

"Circumstantial evidence convicts you, Thayer," Bobby said, coming to the support of his cousin. "You sang; you also fed him. Likewise, you brought him to America. Then wherefore deny?"

"There's no reason I should deny. I like Arlt, and for weeks I had been trying to get him as accompanist, so I gained by the affair. The other fellow didn't, though. He was no musician; but the case interested him. He not only backed Arlt financially, but he hunted up the mother and sister and did no end of nice things for them, the things that count: rolling chairs and extract of beef and all that stuff. He had nothing to make by the transaction."

"Were they properly grateful?" Bobby inquired.

"Yes, to the point of enthusiasm. The mother insisted upon doing his mending all the next winter, and the sister embroidered him a pair of huge antimacassars and a smoking-cap. It sounds funny; but it was grim, earnest tragedy mixed with pathos. He did it all with such tact that the poor creatures never half realized how for a fact they never came into the middle of his life at all. Arlt realizes it, though. That is one of the most pathetic phases of the whole situation. By the way, Dane, you know the fellow, I think."

"I wish I did." Beatrix spoke impetuously. "Plenty of people will give generously, but not many of them are willing to give humanely."

Thayer smiled.

"Old Frau Arlt used to call him her *Lieber Sohn*, and fuss over him as if he were in dire need of her motherly care. He took it just as it was given. The two women lived too quietly to have heard of him. Otto never told them the truth; but outside the house his deference made up for the familiarity at home. It has been a pretty story to watch, and it has meant a comfortable life for two half-starved women."

"Who was the man?" Bobby asked idly.

"Lorimer. Sidney Lorimer."

CHAPTER THREE

Of course, as Bobby Dane had said, with such a name, Thayer's family tree had sprouted in Massachusetts. His Puritanism was hereditary and strong; it tempered the artistic side of his nature, but it could not destroy it. In the musical sense of the word, Cotton Mather Thayer possessed Temperament; but his Temperament was the battle-field where two warring temperaments were at constant strife.

In the year of grace sixteen hundred and thirty-five, Richard Thayer, freeman, landed in America. From Plymouth Rock, he strode straight towards a position of colonial fame. His children and his children's children kept up the family tradition and name until one of them, of a more theological bent than his cousins had been, annulled the custom of his ancestors and named his oldest son for the grim divine, Cotton Mather Thayer, and during the next one hundred and fifty years, Cotton Mathers and Richards had flourished side by side among the Thayers of eastern Massachusetts. They were strong men, one and all, quiet and self-contained in years of peace, grim fighters in seasons of war, and prominent citizens at all times, a godly, gritty, and prosperous race. Of such is the greatness of New England.

Their records, like the records of all good things, were slightly monotonous. They were born into orderly nurseries; they were graduated from the vicissitudes of teething and mumps into orderly, peaceful adolescence. They invariably married the most suitable damsel of their own class, and they passed from an orderly old age through an orderly churchyard into a heaven which the imagination of their surviving kin peopled with orderly ranks of angels, playing gilt harps in perfect accord. Their artistic ideals were bounded by *Coronation* and the pictures in *The New England Primer* and *Godey*. Blackberry shrub, to their minds, was the medium of riotous dissipation.

Under such fostering conditions, ancestral traits strengthened from generation to generation, until the race of Puritan Thayers culminated in one Cotton Mather who was born in the early decades of the last century, a grim deacon, a shrewd lawyer, and the owner of two or three ships which sailed from his own seaport town. Shrewd as he was, however, his logic failed him at one point. When his first child, Cotton Mather Thayer, was a tiny boy, the youngster was allowed and even invited to toddle about the wharves, clinging to the paternal thumb. On the other hand, when the boy Cotton was fourteen, he received a round dozen of canings for lounging about among the shipping. The thirteenth caning was one too many. It was more severe than the others, and it cracked the long-strained situation. The caning occurred in his father's office, after hours, one June night. The *Thankful* was booked to sail, the next morning at eight. When, at eight-ten, it slipped down the harbor, it bore away as cabin-boy and general drudge the stiff and sore, but unrepentant sinner, Cotton Mather Thayer, age fourteen.

His later adventures have little concern with the story of his son's life. He sailed over many seas, he visited many lands, mellowing by contact with many peoples the unyielding temper of his race. The possibility of failure never once entered into his mind. The Thayers always had succeeded, for they always had worked. In consequence, he took it quite as a matter of course that, at twenty-three, he should be commander of the *Presidenta*, stationed in the Baltic for a year of chilly inaction. St. Petersburg was near, and St. Petersburg, as the young commander found, held for him the focal point of the world, in the person of the pretty daughter of one of the court musicians. Twelve years later, while the *Presidenta* was stationed in the Mediterranean, its young captain died, leaving behind him in Russia a fragile wife and a little son who had inherited the name and character of the Thayers, curiously mingled with the artistic, emotional temperament and the rare musical ability of his mother's race.

It was no common combination. Russian art and Puritan morals are equally grim; yet the one yields to every passing emotion, the other is girded up by unyielding strength. Throughout his little boyhood, the child's nature seemed borne hither and thither by these two counter currents in his blood, now passing days of quiet, sturdy self-control, now swept by black gusts of passion which carried all things before them. Then, four years after his father's death, there came two events into his life: his mother's death, and the discovery that he had a voice. The one taught him the meaning of utter, absolute loneliness, for the alien blood of the Thayers had never been able to win many friends in the land of his mother's kin. The other proved to be at once a rudder to guide him over the uncharted future of his life, and an outlet for the pent-up passion within him. His voice was totally untrained, and as yet it broke into all manner of distressing falsetto fragments. Nevertheless, it gave him a cause for living, and it enabled him, the descendant of a taciturn race, to give utterance to the doubts and questionings which accompanied his growth to manhood. Bereft of his mother and without his voice, he might easily have become an ascetic or a criminal.

To a boy of sixteen, trained to a life of strict economy, his slight income from his father's investments seemed enough for his needs, and he felt a boyish disgust when, one day, word came to him that his grandfather had died, leaving him the only heir to the large property laid up by eight generations of Thayers. His grandfather had refused to become reconciled to his son; then why should he assume post-mortem friendship with his son's son? However, by the time he was launched into German student-life, dividing his time fitfully between his university and his music, young Cotton Mather was forced to admit that an ancestral fortune was no despicable addition to the stock in trade of a man starting in life. He only needed to watch the grinding existences of some of his comrades to realize the value of money in shaping a broad artistic career. Instead of wasting his gray matter over details of ways and means, he could let that side of life take care of itself, while he gave his whole attention to developing the best that was in his mind and his voice.

Of course, he was extravagant; of course, he learned, among other things, some of the blacker lessons of the student world. However, the Puritanism of his ancestors stood him in good stead. It enabled him to come into close contact with the seamy side of life; but it decreed that the friction should never leave a sore spot behind it. It only hardened the fibre. When he ended his studies, he knew the world at its best and at its worst, but with this distinction: the best was an integral part of his life; the worst was an alien, a foe to be recognized and downed, however often it should face him.

From Göttingen, where he had met Lorimer casually, Thayer went to Berlin to devote his time entirely to music. Lorimer joined him there, more because he had nothing to call him back to America than because he had anything to call him to Berlin. During the next winter, the two men, as unlike as men could be, had shared a bachelor apartment, the one working industriously, the other playing just as industriously. It was during this winter that Lorimer had come into contact with the Arlts. It was during this winter also that Thayer finally decided to give up his other plans and make his profession centre in his voice. He had battled against the idea with the fervor of a race to whom "the stage" offered no distinction between vaudeville and grand opera, but inclined to the characteristics of the one and the scope of the other. For years, he had fought against the temptation; he yielded, one night, during the second act of *Faust*, and, in after time, he could always identify the chord which had punctuated his decision. Three hours later, he was studying that fraction of Baedeker which concerns itself with Italy.

He was in Italy for two years. Then he went back to Berlin for another year of grinding work, of passing discouragements, and of ultimate success. There had been many and many a day when his pluck had failed him, when he had questioned whether his voice was really good, whether, after all, it were possible to make an artist out of gritty Puritan stock; whether, in fact, he was not a thing of fibre, rather than a man of temperament. His progress was great; but his ideals kept pace with it.

It was one dazzling June morning when he took his final lesson. He had gone onward and upward until, for months, he had been in the hands of the *maestro* universally acknowledged to be the dean of his art. The *maestro* was an old man and chary of his words; yet even he was stirred to enthusiasm.

"My son, it is time for you to go," he said, as he rose from the piano and took Thayer's hands into his own fragile, elderly fingers. "I can teach you nothing more. It is now for you to work out your own reputation. Not much more of life is left in me; but, before it is ended, I shall hear your name spoken, both often and with praise. While I live, my house will hold a welcome to you. *Auf wiedersehen!*"

As Thayer went out into the sunshine, the glitter and the brightness of it all, of the day and of the future, dazzled him and made him afraid. Then of a sudden the blood of the Thayers, in abeyance during those mad, sad, glad years of study and of striving, asserted itself again. Obeying its behest, he turned abruptly from the street where he was seeking the impresario to whom his master had sent him. In that instant, he turned his back for many a long month upon opera and upon all that followed in its train.

One clean, cold night in mid-February, Thayer came down the steps of his club, where he had been dining with Bobby Dane. At the foot of the steps he halted long enough to button his coat to the chin and pull his hat over his eyes, preparatory to facing the cutting wind. Then, turning southward, he went striding away down the Avenue with the vigorous, alert tread of the well-fed, contented man. It was still early, so early that the pavements were dotted with theatre-going groups. He strode through and beyond them, along the lower end of the Avenue, and came under the arch, standing in chill, austere dignity at the edge of the wind-swept square. Over its fretted surface the electric lights shone coldly, and the deserted benches beyond brought to Thayer, fresh from the glow and good-fellowship of the club, a sudden depressing sense of his own aloofness from his kind. The club and Bobby were incidental points of contact, pleasant, but not permanent. Like the arch, he was alone, outside the rushing life of the busy town, something to be watched and commented upon, but never destined to be really in the heart of things. Bobby was a part of it, and Bobby had held out to him a welcoming hand. He had taken the hand, and had dropped it again. It was of no use. He did not belong. The sensation was not a new one to him. He had met it before and in many places. It came to him suddenly and unbidden, and it lay, a chilly weight, over all his consciousness. It always left him wondering whether he would ever become fully adjusted to his environment, whether it would ever be possible for him to come into perfect contact with his fellow-men.

As if the depression had brought with it a physical chill, he shook his broad shoulders and plunged his hands into the side pockets of his overcoat. Then, facing westward, he went on for a block or two and stopped at the door of a shabby boarding-house.

"Mr. Arlt?" he said to the maid, in brief interrogation.

She nodded and stood aside to let him pass. Thayer's tread on the dim stairway showed his familiarity with the place, as did the prompt calling of his name which answered his knock.

Without laying down his pipe, Arlt rose to greet his guest.

"You were so late that I was afraid you were not coming."

Thayer took off his fur-lined coat and tossed it into a chair.

"Haven't you learned that I always get around?" he asked. "I was dining with a friend, and we took things lazily."

"And now you expect to sing?" Arlt's accent was rebuking.

"Yes. I walked down here to get myself into condition. How is it? Are you feeling nervous over the prospect?"

Arlt had seated himself at the grand piano which completely filled one end of the dreary room. Now he drew a protesting arpeggio from the black keys and shook his head.

"Oh, that is a terrible woman, that Mrs. Lloyd Avalons! She was here again, to-day, to tell me about the programme. What does she know of music? She refuses the Haydn Variations and demands a Liszt Rhapsodie. If you are not firm with her, she will end by making you sing *The Holy City* with a flute obligato."

Thayer laughed unfeelingly.

"She is a Vandal, Arlt; but the world will be at her musicale, they tell me; and you will find it a good place to make your bow to an American public. Mrs. Dana told me, over in Berlin, that Mrs. Lloyd Avalons gave the best private recitals in New York."

"What does she know about music?" Arlt grumbled.

"Nothing, apparently; but the new-rich must have some sort of a fad, if they are to make themselves count for anything, and people will go to hear good music, even when they know it is a mere social bribe. Hofman could fill a Bowery dance-hall with the elect; you only have to lead them to the latest architectural vagary on Fifth Avenue. They are bound to be there, for, even while they scoff, they like to keep an eye on Mrs. Lloyd Avalons for fear she may prove to be worth knowing after they have snubbed her; so play your best. It may lead to other engagements to come."

"And the Liszt Rhapsodie?" he asked mournfully.

"Bad, I admit."

"It is detestable. The Rhapsodies are the forlorn hope of artists who have failed on Beethoven."

"Not so bad as that. Still, there's a way of escape. Announce to your audience that, by request, you are changing the number from Liszt to Haydn. I do request it most earnestly."

The boy looked up in admiring relief.

"How is it that such ideas come to you, Mr. Thayer?"

"My Yankee blood, Arlt. Now shall we run over my songs?"

It was characteristic of Thayer that, in consenting to make his American début at the recital of Mrs. Lloyd Avalons, he had insisted upon the condition that he should choose his own assisting artist. How Mrs. Lloyd Avalons had heard of him in the first place was a mystery which he had made no effort to solve. From the testimony of several members of the American colony in Berlin, it appeared that all New York and half of Boston had heard of Mrs. Lloyd Avalons, who, for three or four seasons past, had been using her really choice musicales as a species of knocker upon the portal of New York society. By this time, she had passed the portal and was disporting herself in the vestibule, with one toe resting upon the sacred threshold. Socially, she was as yet impossible; but her recitals had won the reputation of being among the choicest tidbits of the season's musical feast, for she made up in money what she lacked in artistic sense, and, thanks to her agent, she had been able to discover certain new stars before they rose above the horizon. For this reason it was a distinct honor, Thayer was told, to be bidden to sing for Mrs. Lloyd Avalons, and therefore Thayer had promptly made up his mind that Arlt also should have a hearing upon this occasion. The boy already had decided to come to America. Thayer realized with regret how cold a welcome the country of his own ancestors was accustomed to extend to struggling young musicians. Arlt had genius; but he lacked both influence and initiative. The fight would be a long one, and Arlt's conquest would be at the expense of many a wound. Teutons are not necessarily pachyderms, and Arlt was sensitive to a rare degree.

As Arlt's fingers dropped from the keys at the close of *Valentine's* song of farewell, Thayer laughed suddenly.

"It is rather contrary to custom to be accompanied by the star of the evening, Arlt. I suppose I ought to have hunted up somebody else; but these other fellows make frightful work of my accompaniments. They hurry till they get me out of breath, and then they take advantage of the moment to drown me out. I'd like a baton, only I should beat the accompanist with it, before I was half through a programme."

The boy's color came.

"When another man accompanies you, I shall be dead, or incapable," he returned briefly. "I do not forget."

"Nor I. But do you also remember the last time we did this in Germany?"

"At my home? To Katarina?"

Thayer nodded.

"It is my song, you know. I am superstitious about it."

"Mr. Lorimer was there, that night."

"Oh, that reminds me, Arlt, I heard, to-night, that Lorimer was engaged."

"Mr. Lorimer?"

"Yes, to a Miss Dane. It is only just announced, to-day. I was dining with her cousin and he told me."

"She must be good. I hope she is also strong of character," the boy said, with a curiously deliberate accent which seemed characteristic of him. "He is a good man and a kind one; but he needs a steadying hand. I shall write to the mother and Katarina."

"Will they like the news?"

"Why not? Mr. Lorimer is their friend, and they will be glad of any happiness which shall come to him. To the mother, he is like a son, for she is simple-hearted and knows nothing of the world. To Katarina, he is like a god."

"But gods don't usually marry," Thayer suggested whimsically, as he took up his coat.

However, Arlt was ready for him.

"Zeus did, and Homer tells us how he quarrelled with his wife.'"

"Lorimer never will quarrel; he is too easy-going. By the way, you met Miss Dane at the Stanley recital. Do you remember her?"

Arlt's lips straightened thoughtfully.

"A tall lady in brown furs, who knew how to praise without making a fool of herself?" he queried.

"That is the one. I should judge that Lorimer has been making a systematic campaign ever since he met her, three months ago, and that, after all, it came suddenly in the end. Dane was noncommittal; but I think he doesn't like Lorimer any too well. Good-night, Arlt. We'll rehearse again, Wednesday morning; meanwhile, stick to your Haydn." And Thayer went away, out into the cold, crisp air, which greeted him now with all its tonic force.

Arlt's simple, boyish loyalty and lack of self-analysis always put him into good-humor. It was as infectious as the jovial temper of Bobby Dane, Thayer reflected enviously, with a sudden memory of the idle talk over their dinner. Strange what had put him on his nerves afterwards! Then his thoughts flew to Lorimer, and he wondered how his old chum would bear the harness of domestic living. Perhaps it was just as well that no idea crossed his mind of how far his story told to Beatrix Dane, the Monday before, had had a share in shaping the decision which was to change the whole character of her life.

The question of one's accountability for others is rarely an edifying subject of meditation.

CHAPTER FOUR

"It isn't so easy to say airy nothings to an artist, when you know him behind the scenes," Beatrix said, suddenly shifting the talk back to the point of departure.

"Talk philosophy, then," Bobby returned.

"But I must say something to him, after he gets through singing; and now that I have seen him, three or four times, I can't launch into a sea of platitudes."

"I thought women could always go to sea in a platitude. It is as leaky as a sieve, and not half so likely to upset and leave one floating without any support at all."

Sally laughed outright.

"Beware of Bobby, when he turns metaphorical! He suggests a second-hand curio shop."

Lorimer glanced up at her, with a whimsical smile twisting his lips.

"Your own rhetoric isn't above reproach, Miss Van Osdel. But has it ever occurred to you that Young America has abandoned its sieve for a man of war? I met a callow junior from Harvard, the other day, and by way of making polite conversation, I asked him to suggest a clever subject for a debate. He promptly told me that at his eating club they had been discussing the origins of morality."

Bobby whistled, to the huge delight of the butler. That factotum revelled in the pranks of "Master Bobby" who had upset his dignity at least once a week for the past fifteen years.

"In our time we took our pleasures less sadly, Lorimer. What are we all coming to?"

"To congenital senility."

"That is nothing more nor less than the frugal trick of making both ends meet," Sally interpolated.

"But what shall I say to Mr. Thayer?" Beatrix reiterated.

"That it is a pleasant evening."

"That you hope he isn't very tired with singing so much," Bobby and Sally suggested in the same breath.

Beatrix made a little gesture of scorn.

"It is your turn, Mr. Lorimer. You know him better than the rest of us. What shall you say to him?"

"I know him so well that I rarely talk to him about his singing," Lorimer replied, with sudden gravity. "Thayer is too large a man to smack his lips over sugar-plums. He knows exactly what I think of his voice, that it is one of the best baritone voices I have ever heard. He also knows that I am perfectly aware of the fact when he sings unusually badly or unusually well. Under those conditions, there is no especial need of our discussing the matter. One can have reservations with one's friends, you know." As he spoke, his eyes met those of Beatrix, and a smile lighted his gravity.

At a first glance, Sidney Lorimer produced the impression of being a remarkably handsome man. The second glance, while it strengthened the impression, nevertheless set one wondering what had created it. His figure, his features, his coloring were all good, yet they were in no way remarkable. A wiry, nervous, clean-cut man, with brown hair and eyes, a slim, straight nose, and a well-set head, he would have commanded little attention had it not been for the nameless stamp set upon him by his training at an English public-school. It is impossible to analyze this stamp, yet it exists and insists upon recognition. Political life had called the elder Lorimer to England, and he had judged it better to take his only child with him and drop him into Eton than to leave him in America and send him to St. Paul's. He did it as a matter of convenience, not of theory; but when his boy was ready for a Yale diploma, the father confessed to himself that he was pleased with the result of the experiment. Young Lorimer would never be an important factor in the world's development; but he was an uncommonly attractive fellow, and could hold his own in any position where chance would be likely to place him. Only his lower lip betrayed the fact that his mother had been a woman of uncurbed nerves.

It was the evening of the twentieth, and Lorimer was distinctly nervous. He liked Arlt and was anxious for his success; but his anxiety for Arlt was as nothing in comparison with that which he felt for Thayer, to whom he gave the adoration that a weak man sometimes offers to one immeasurably his superior. Probably Lorimer's whole life would contain no better year than the one he had spent with Thayer in Berlin. Thayer's influence was strongly good, and Lorimer was of plastic material. It is doubtful whether Lorimer realized this influence;

yet he was genuinely delighted to have Thayer within easy reach once more, genuinely wishful to have Thayer's American début such an unqualified success that hereafter he would regard New York as his professional home.

Lorimer rarely was garrulous; he was unusually silent during the long drive to the Lloyd Avalons's. It was his first introduction to the pseudo-fashionable world, for his own family had been of conservative stock, and Beatrix and Bobby had been the first of the Danes to break down the barriers of their own exclusive set. To be sure, he realized that in a city like New York it was quite possible for circles of equal choiceness to exist tangent to each other, yet in mutual ignorance of one another; but his years abroad in slower-moving countries had not prepared him for the countless agile performers clambering up and down over the social trapeze. In his father's day, society had stood on an elevated platform and watched the performers as they played leap-frog on the ground. The performers had been as agile then as now; but their agility had been free from any danger of a tumble. Between the ground and the platform, there is no place of permanent rest. One must keep moving, or else be pushed to the ground.

As a rule, people forgot that there was a Mr. Lloyd Avalons. He was a little man with an imperial, and a total incapacity for telling the truth. In that, he was inferior to his wife in point of social evolution, for she had learned, from certain episodes which still filled her with mortification, that fibbing was bad form. To Mrs. Lloyd Avalons, her husband was a mere cipher. Placed before her, he added nothing to her value; placed after and in the background, he multiplied her importance tenfold. There were certain privileges accruing to a woman with a husband, certain immunities that followed in the train of matrimony. Mrs. Lloyd Avalons was quite willing to include the word *obey* in the marriage service; she had a distinct choice in regard to whom it should refer.

To-night, Lloyd Avalons stood slightly in the rear of the elbow of his wife who, resplendent in pale gray velvet and emeralds, was welcoming her guests on the threshold of the music-room. Her gray eyes were shining with a greenish light that matched the emeralds, for her lips were set in a conventional smile, and there must be some escape for her delight, as she counted over the tale of guests and recognized individuals of many a named species from the garden of society. All in all, this was the best success she had as yet attained.

She greeted Beatrix effusively, and cast a coy glance at Lorimer while she murmured a few words of congratulation. Then she fell a victim to one of Bobby's quibbles, and while she was struggling to see the point of his joke, the others made their escape.

"At least, the architect knew what he was about," Lorimer remarked to Beatrix, as they took their seats. "Thayer can't complain of the acoustic effects of the place."

"When have you seen him?"

"Just before dinner. He was in superb voice then, and a fairly good mood."

"Isn't he always?" she questioned idly, as she nodded to an acquaintance in the next row of chairs.

"Not always. As a rule, he is the best-tempered fellow in the world. Once in a while, though, he wraps himself up in his dignity and stalks about like an Indian brave in his best Navajo blanket. Nobody ever knows what is the reason, nor when he will go off into a Mood. It makes him an uncertain quantity. For my part, I would rather a man would swear and get it over with." Lorimer spoke easily. Unlike Thayer, he never collided with the angles of his own temperament.

"What does it do to his singing?"

"Depends on one's taste. I like it, myself, as I like a high-flavored cheese. People who pin their faith to Mendelssohn might be a little over-powered. Fact is, there is a strange streak in Thayer's make-up. I can't account for him at all."

"What is the use of trying? Aren't one's friends immune from analysis?"

"I don't care to try. I don't want to account for him; he is too large for that. I wish you might know him; but you never will. He's not a woman's man in the least."

Beatrix was silent for a moment. Involuntarily she was making a swift comparison of the way in which the two men spoke of each other. Lorimer's praise had been full of half-suppressed reservations. Thayer had made no reservations, he had scarcely uttered a word of praise, yet his hastily-drawn picture of Lorimer's connection with the Arlts had proved a determining factor in her life. It had been a new phase of Lorimer's character which Thayer had presented. It had revealed him in a new light and one infinitely more likable than any she had yet known. The Lorimer she had met, had been fascinating and a bit snobbish. The friend of the Arlts was altogether lovable. It takes greater tact and staying power to make friends outside one's social grade than in it. People suspect the motives of those who are crossing the boundaries between caste and caste; yet the Arlts had trusted Lorimer completely.

Beatrix had remained thoughtful for some time after Thayer's departure. Lorimer had called, that same night. His coming had been unexpected; it had taken Beatrix off her guard. She had been unfeignedly glad to see him, for his ten-days' absence from her life had been unprecedented in their acquaintance. The world is wide, yet, owing to some strange law of attraction, one invariably seems to meet the same people everywhere. Beatrix had greeted Lorimer more eagerly than she had been aware. She had tried in vain to keep the fact of the Forbes supper uppermost in her mind. Instead, it slid into the background, and its place had been taken by the thought of Lorimer's probable feelings when he received the smoking cap from the hands of Katarina Arlt. And the evening had hurried away from her. When it had gone, she had realized with a sudden shock that her girlhood was ended. She was the plighted bride of Sidney Lorimer, and, distrustful of her own mental grasp of the fact, she had ruthlessly waked up her mother to tell her what had occurred. Later, she had not understood the motive which had led her to her mother's room. As a rule, she was self-reliant, and adjusted herself to a crisis without caring to talk it over. For the once, however, she felt the need of being strengthened by the enthusiastic delight of Mrs. Dane whose sentimental hopes had centered in Lorimer from the hour of his introduction to her only child.

All this had passed in review through Beatrix's mind, and it seemed long to her since Lorimer's last words, when he said,--

"Don't think I am depreciating Thayer, Beatrix. He is one of the finest fellows who ever came out of the Creator's hands. In his worst moods, he is away ahead of most of the men one meets. Some day, I hope you may know him for what he really is."

There was true generosity underlying Lorimer's frank words. He was still smarting from his contact with Thayer, that afternoon, for Thayer had heard of a dinner at the club, on the previous night, and had spoken a quiet warning. It was only such a warning as he had given, a dozen times before; he knew just how Lorimer would resent it, then accept it, and it would have made no difference to him, could he have foreseen that, in his resentment, Lorimer's words to Beatrix would be slightly tinged with aloes. It is not certain that, foreseeing, he would have cared. Beatrix was nothing to him; of Lorimer he was strangely fond.

Beatrix had felt some curiosity as to the effect Thayer's voice might have upon her. Familiarity in all truth does breed contempt, and a second hearing often proves a disappointment. For Lorimer's sake, she was anxious to enjoy the recital, and she drew a quick, nervous breath as Thayer, followed by Arlt, came striding out across the little stage with the same unconscious ease with which he had crossed her parlor, the week before. As he waited for Arlt to seat himself, he glanced about the room, his practised eye measuring its size and the probable nature of his audience. For an instant, his glance rested upon Beatrix and Lorimer, and he gave a slight smile of recognition. Then his shoulders straightened and he came to attention, as Arlt struck the opening chord of his accompaniment.

He had chosen to begin his programme, that night, with the *Infelice* for, in spite of its Verdiism, it had been a favorite of his old master in Berlin. Before he had sung a dozen notes, Beatrix, bending forward, was listening with parted lips and flushing cheeks. Of Thayer as a man who had dallied with one of her cups of tea, she took no account; but his voice, sweet and flexible, was tugging at her nerves and setting them vibrating with its note of passionate sadness. Then, gathering power and intensity, it swept its hearers along upon its furious tempest; yet, as she listened, Beatrix felt herself inspired for, underneath it all, there was the same throbbing, insistent note which seemed to assure her that the singer had hoped and lost and fought and conquered, that he knew all about it, himself.

Lorimer nodded contentedly at the stage, as Thayer ended his song.

"That's all right; but they would better save their strength, for he never gives an encore for the first number. What do you think of Thayer now, Beatrix?"

She caught her breath sharply.

"That I should be a better woman, if I could hear him sing often."

"There's something in what you say. He makes me feel it, too. I never have heard him sing better, though he always does that song well. He told me once that he felt possessed with the spirit of his own grandfather, whenever he started it. From all signs, his grandfather must have been an intolerable old person to get on with, if he could rage in that fashion."

"Possibly he had occasion." Beatrix forced herself to speak lightly, though it was an effort for her to resume the accent and manner which befitted the place.

"Perhaps. He was a Russian musician with a young wife. Now for the Schubert group! Thayer's reputation is made, though; he can sing through his nose now, and they will think it a beautiful manifestation of individual genius. I only hope that Arlt will do one tenth as well."

It proved that Arlt did fully six tenths as well, and was applauded to the echo. To the undiscerning ear, he won even more than his share of applause; but Beatrix, her nerves still tense from *The Erl-King*, felt a difference in the quality of the welcome to the two musicians. The critical few were impartial, and in the case of Arlt they led a wavering fugue of the uncritical many. Arlt was young, small and insignificant. His tailor was not an artist, and Arlt was too palpably conscious that his coat tails demanded respectful care. Society applauded Arlt with punctilious courtesy; but it promptly took Thayer to its bosom and caressed him with enthusiasm.

Late in the evening, Beatrix brought her father to the corner where Thayer, with Arlt beside him, was still holding a sort of court, and the four of them were talking quietly when Mrs. Stanley came pushing her way towards them.

"I must add my word of congratulation, Mr. Thayer," she said, as she graciously offered him a pudgy bundle of white kid fingers. "You have made a wonderful success, and it won't be long before you have New York at your feet."

Thayer glanced down at his patent leather shoes.

"It would be a good deal in the way, Mrs. Stanley. Let us hope it will stay where it belongs," he answered gravely.

"How ungrateful you artists are! But I shall always be so glad and proud to think that your first song in New York was in my house."

"But it wasn't."

Her face fell.

"I thought--Wasn't that your first recital? I am sure you said--"

His smile went no further than his lips, for his clear gray eyes appeared to be taking her mental and spiritual measure, with some little disappointment at the result.

"It was my first recital, Mrs. Stanley; but not my first song. I sang German folk songs to Arlt's landlady, half the afternoon before. You remember Mr. Arlt, I think."

She glanced around with a carelessness which ignored the hand that the boy shyly extended towards her.

"Oh, yes, very pleased," she said vaguely. Then, with a resumption of her former manner, she turned back to Thayer. "And I thought you promised to drop in for a cup of tea, some Thursday, Mr. Thayer."

Beatrix was deaf to his answer. She had turned to Arlt who, scarlet with hurt and anger, stood alone in his corner by the piano.

"Mr. Arlt," she said gayly; "it is very warm here, and I know where they keep the frappé. Shall we leave my father here, and run off in search of some goodies? You ought to be hungry, after playing for two hours. Come!"

And Arlt, surprised at the sudden winning intonations which had crept into her voice, dodged around the portly back of Mrs. Stanley and followed Beatrix out of the room. For the moment, the haughty woman had changed to a jovial, friendly girl, no more awe-inspiring than Katarina, in spite of her wonderful gown and the fluffy white thing in her hair; and the artist, in his turn, changed into a normal hungry boy, as he followed her away.

So absorbed were they in each other that they failed to see Bobby Dane who met them upon the threshold, on his way to join the group they had just left.

"Beg pardon, Thayer; but can I speak to you for a moment?" he said abruptly.

His uncle turned to Mrs. Stanley with old-fashioned pomposity.

"May I have the pleasure of taking you to the dining-room?" he asked.

"What is it, Dane?" Thayer asked, as soon as they were alone, for Bobby's face showed that something was amiss.

"It's Lorimer in the smoking-room. That beast of a Lloyd Avalons has opened a perfect bar in there, and--and Lorimer is making a bit of a cad of himself," Bobby confessed reluctantly. "I tried to get him away; but he wouldn't come, and I thought perhaps you could start him. It's not that he is drunk, only he is talking rather too much, and I want to get him off before Beatrix gets wind of it. You know girls--"

"I know," Thayer assented gravely. "I'll see what I can do with him."

CHAPTER FIVE

"You musicians make me deadly weary," Bobby proclaimed, from his favorite rostrum of the hearthrug.

"Is that the reason you are trying to sit on them, Bobby?" his cousin asked. "You'll find an easy chair just as restful to you and a good deal more so to the musician."

Bobby waved her remark aside.

"Don't interrupt me, Beatrix. I have things I wish to say."

"Very likely; but it is barely possible that somebody else also may have things he wishes to say, and can't, because you talk so much."

"Sally is busy eating bonbons, and Thayer would much better wait till I get through his indictment. He'll need all his voice to defend himself."

Sally glanced up.

"Go on, Bobby," she said encouragingly. "The sooner it is over, the better."

"Thank you. Then I have the floor. Thayer, I never believe in talking about people behind their backs, so I look you squarely in the eye and ask you if you ever realize that you don't amount to much, after all."

"Who told you?"

"Nobody. I evolved it."

"I didn't know you were a critic."

"I'm not, nor yet an interpreting artist. I create."

"What, I should like to know!" This was from Sally.

"Scareheads. I do them. If that's not creating, I should like to know what is. They never have any connection with facts."

"What is your grievance?" Thayer asked languidly.

"I was just getting to that. As I say, I create. You only interpret. I don't know as it counts that you don't try to interpret my scareheads, though some of them would make stunning fugues. Take the last one, for instance: *Billions at Stake: Potato Corner in Prospect.* You could work up something fine from that, Thayer. Think of the chest tones you could throw into the single word *Potato*!"

"Bobby, you are growing discursive," his cousin reminded him.

"No; it is only my rhetorical method. I shall bring you up with a round turn, before you know it. Well, granted that we represent the two classes, the creative and the interpretive, which is the greater?"

"How can we tell, unless you stand back to back?" Sally inquired.

But by this time, Bobby was fairly launched.

"The fact is, you singers and players have a smug little fashion of forgetting that there is a composer back of you. You don't sing extempore, Thayer, make up the song as you go along. You're nothing more than a species of elocutionist, you know, trying to show the people who weren't on the spot what the composer really did when he created the thing."

"Animated phonograph records, in short?" Thayer suggested.

"Yes, if you choose to call it that. Of course you count for something, else every composer could make a set of records and dispense with his interpreting artist once for all. But you fellows honestly do make an awful fuss about yourselves; now don't you?"

"Bobby!" Beatrix protested.

"Oh, yes; but I'm not meaning anything personal," Bobby responded amicably. "We know that Thayer's voice is beyond all odds the best we have heard for a three years. How do you do it, Thayer? You look as calm as a Dutch dolly; but you manage to tear us all to bits. Even I felt sanctified at your recital, and Miss Van Osdel's lashes were freighted with unshed tears."

"That must be one of your next week's scareheads," she objected. "I never cry in public where there are electric lights, Mr. Thayer; it's horribly unbecoming to most women. But I did have to say a nonsense rhyme over to myself, to keep steady."

"Yes, I taught you that trick," Beatrix asserted suddenly. "Lear is very soothing in an emotional crisis. *The Rubáiyát* for gooseflesh and Lear for tears is my rule. *The Jumblies* carried me safely through the fifth act of *Cyrano*. But go on, Bobby. We are nearly ready to change the subject."

"Now take that recital of yours," Bobby pursued meditatively. "You were there to interpret Schubert and Franz and those fellows; but nobody is talking about Schubert and Franz, to-day. It is all Thayer, Cotton Mather Thayer, Baritone. It's all right enough. You did them awfully well; but there's the Them in the background, and it's not decent to forget Them."

Thayer laughed good-naturedly. It was impossible to take offence at the mock seriousness of Bobby's harangue. Furthermore, it held its own grain of truth, even though the grain was buried in an infinite amount of chaff.

"I do occasionally remember that there was a composer," he suggested; "and, in case of the dead ones, you need somebody to sing them."

"Ye-es," Bobby replied grudgingly; "and in case of the live ones, too, sometimes. I have an idea that you make a good deal better noise out of it than most of these old duffers would do. It is only that you take all the glory for the whole business. The newsboys on the street corners have no right to take the credit for my scareheads."

"They are a self-respecting race, Bobby; they don't want to."

"How unkind of you, Sally! But the cases are analogous. And my final point, aside from professional jealousy, is the economy of time. You grub longer over learning to sing a song than it takes the composer to write it, and, when you're through, you've only reproduced somebody else's ideas. Why can't you be original? Next time you feel musically inclined, just say to yourself, 'Go to, now! Let us create!' It won't take a bit longer, and really it's not hard to do. I know, because, you see, I do it."

"Bravo, Bobby! I am delighted to hear that you ever do anything."

At the new voice, Bobby whirled around and bowed himself into a right angle, while Beatrix rose and crossed the room to greet the guest.

"Miss Gannion! What joy to see you!"

Thayer's Russian blood received swift impressions; his Puritanism made him weigh and measure with careful deliberation. Now, as he bowed in acknowledgment of the introduction, he was conscious that in Margaret Gannion he was meeting a woman who would bear either test. She seemed to him one of the most strongly individual women he had ever met; yet at the same time he had a comfortable sense of an infinite number of points of mental contact. Later, he was destined to learn that this sense was not imparted to himself alone. Margaret Gannion was tangent to many lives.

"What is the discussion?" she inquired, as she seated herself.

"No discussion at all, Miss Gannion. Bobby is doing a monologue on music, and the rest of us can't get a word in edgewise."

"Have you joined the ranks of the musicians, Bobby?"

"Yes, or the angels," Sally responded for him. "Nothing else could have such a fatal facility for harping on one string."

"I was so sorry to lose your recital, Mr. Thayer," Miss Gannion said, after a while, as she turned her steady brown eyes on the young man. "I was in Boston, that week, and I am told that I missed one of the treats of the season. When am I to have another chance of hearing you?"

Thayer hesitated for a moment, while his gray eyes met the brown ones that seemed to be taking his mental measure. Apparently both were satisfied with what they saw, for they exchanged a smile of sudden understanding. Then Thayer's face grew grave.

"Whenever you wish," he replied quietly.

"Does that mean you will sing to me, myself? I should never have dared hope for that."

"Why not? That is, if you will let me bring Arlt with me. I dislike to force him upon people; but he is the only accompanist I really enjoy."

Beatrix looked up with a laugh.

"You never asked if you might bring him here, Mr. Thayer."

Suddenly he rose.

"May I take that as a hint, Miss Dane? I can play a few accompaniments after a fashion." And, without waiting for the response which was sure to come, he crossed the room to the piano.

He sang Schubert's *Haiden Röslein* and an American song or two. The hush over the room deepened, as the last words fell on the stillness,--

"Oh barren gain! Oh bitter loss! I kiss each bead, and strive at last to learn To kiss the cross--"

And, in the midst of the stillness, he rose and quietly returned to his old place by the fire.

It was long before anyone spoke. Then even Miss Gannion's level voice jarred upon the silence.

"You have a wonderful gift in your keeping, Mr. Thayer," was all she said.

But Beatrix was silent, her eyes fixed on the glowing coals. At length she roused herself with an effort. Reverie was not permissible for a hostess on her reception day. She came out of hers, to find that the conversation had broken into duets. At one side of the table, Bobby and Sally were sparring vivaciously; at the other, Miss Gannion and Thayer had fallen into quiet talk about certain common friends and about the simplest method of helping Arlt to gain the professional recognition he deserved and needed.

"I'm not potent at all," Miss Gannion said regretfully. "I only know people who are, and they are not always receptive in their minds. Still, I may be able to do something, and he made a good impression at Mrs. Lloyd Avalons's recital. In the meantime, bring him to my home, some evening soon. Friday is my day; but, if you don't mind--"

Thayer understood her.

"Arlt will like it a great deal better, and so shall I. He is a shy fellow, and he never shows at his best, when too many people are about."

Miss Gannion's face betrayed her relief. She had not meant to seem inhospitable; neither had she desired apparently to be scheming for a free recital. It was a precarious matter, this establishing social relations with a really great artist who had just expressed his willingness to sing in private life. Miss Gannion's acquaintance was large and of many lines; but Thayer was a new species to her, and she had felt somewhat at a loss how to treat him, as artist or as mere man. Thayer's answer inclined her to the latter alternative.

"What about Saturday, then?" she asked. "I shall be at home, that night."

"Please ask me, Miss Gannion," Bobby entreated.

Miss Gannion shook her head.

"No; you are too much in evidence, Bobby. You would distract my mind from Mr. Arlt, and this is his party, you know. Even Mr. Thayer is subordinate. But, Beatrix child, where is Mr. Lorimer? I thought surely I should find him here, to-day. I've not congratulated him yet. That was one thing that brought me here."

Beatrix flushed a little.

"Mr. Lorimer was called to Washington, last Thursday," she answered so evenly that no one would have suspected the wondering annoyance which his hasty note of explanation had caused her.

"Then he was here for your recital." Miss Gannion turned back to Thayer once more. "Didn't someone tell me you were old friends, Mr. Thayer? It must have been a very exhilarating night for him, this American début of yours."

For the space of a minute, out of her four hearers, three were holding their breath. Under the promise of the strictest secrecy, Bobby had confided to Sally the story of the scene in the smoking-room; and, like two conspirators, they had spent a long evening in stealthy discussion of the best way to keep the matter from the ears of Beatrix. Sally liked Lorimer; Bobby detested him, yet to neither of them had the matter seemed of quite sufficient importance to justify a broken engagement, and they were too well acquainted with the strict code of Beatrix Dane to doubt what would be the outcome of the affair, if the facts were to reach her ears. Sally was less mature, less aware of the danger inherent in the situation, less strong in her condemnation of what she termed "friskiness." Bobby, with a shrug of his shoulders, admitted that a man should not be condemned for a first offence, that there was plenty of time to watch for a repetition of the affair, to warn Beatrix then and to allow her to take her own course as seemed good to her. Meanwhile, there was no use in disturbing her for nothing. It might be a single slip, such as all men are liable to make. Of course, as Sally argued, Lorimer had been under strong excitement, that evening, partly by reason of his own newly-announced engagement, partly by reason of the brilliant success of his friend. Lloyd Avalons was just the man to take advantage of such a situation, and to think it a huge piece of humorous hospitality to throw Lorimer off his guard. Lloyd Avalons had never joined the camp of the prohibitionists, himself, and he saw no reason for staying the appetites of his guests. To his mind, that Sidney Lorimer could drink too much wine in his house presupposed a certain intimacy. At least, if the incident were to be mentioned, their names were bound to be bracketed with each other. Like his wife, Lloyd Avalons possessed his social ambitions.

In the most accurate use of the words, Lorimer had not been drunk, only intoxicated. When Thayer, with Bobby at his side, had appeared in the door of the smoking-room, Lorimer had been more flushed, more garrulous than was his wont, more inclined to the French doctrine of equality and fraternity. In some moods, he would not have tolerated the arm of Lloyd Avalons which now rested across the back of his chair.

The scene lasted only for an instant. Thayer went into the room, accepted a dozen hot hands whose owners were trying rather incoherently to congratulate him upon his success, waved aside the wine offered him, and, with a word of excuse, bent down and spoke quietly to Lorimer.

"Beg pardon, Mr. Avalons," he said shortly; "but I have a message for Mr. Lorimer. He is needed on business, and I shall have to take him away. Please give my good-night to Mrs. Avalons. My cab is waiting, and I can set Lorimer down at his club." And, with a bow, he had left the room, with Lorimer sullenly following at his heels.

In Lorimer's room, Thayer broke the silence which had lasted during their drive along the brilliantly-lighted Avenue. He had watched his companion's face keenly and with an understanding born of similar scenes, and he knew it would not be well to use many words. However, as he was leaving Lorimer, he turned back.

"This is once too often, Lorimer," he said briefly. "You've somebody besides yourself to think of now. If I were in your place, I would have important business call me to Washington, in the morning, and I would stay down there for a few days. It will give you time to think things over, and find out just where you stand."

CHAPTER SIX

Miss Gannion nestled luxuriously back into the depths of her easy chair.

"Do you know, Mr. Thayer, it is a very wonderful experience, this having a species of court musician?"

He laughed the silent laugh she liked so well. It came from between close-shut teeth; but it lighted his whole face.

"As wonderful as it is to have a good listener who always understands and rarely praises?" he asked.

Under her thin, middle-aged skin, the flush rose to her cheeks, turning them to the dainty likeness of youth.

"You say very pleasant things."

"True ones. If this keeps on, I shall begin using you as critic for all my new songs."

"Like the fabled dog? I wish you would. But, truly, I am not joking. You are quite spoiling me for my usual diet of recitals. Do you realize that, for the past two months, you have sung to me on an average of two hours a week?"

Thayer smiled contentedly down at her, as he sat by the piano, with one muscular arm thrown across the rack.

"Well, what of it?" he inquired.

"Nothing, except that people say you are refusing engagements."

"A fellow must have a little time to enjoy his friends," he returned coolly. "I can't be expected to sing, six nights a week."

"Your logic betrays your artistic nature. You have sung at five recitals, this week. This is the sixth night; but you've not been silent."

"You know you wanted to hear *Faust* sung again."

"Yes, and so did Mrs. Stanley want you to sing at her house."

He looked up sharply.

"Who told you?"

"Mr. Arlt."

"Arlt shouldn't tell tales. But I had three good reasons for refusing: I don't like Mrs. Stanley; she doesn't treat Arlt as well as she treats her pug dog, and moreover you had asked me to dinner. I never sing after a good dinner."

"But you mustn't refuse engagements."

"I didn't. I kept one."

"Engagements to sing, I mean. You seem to forget that you are a star."

"All the more reason I should stop twinkling now and then. I can't be on duty, the whole time. Besides, Miss Gannion," he rose from the piano and came forward to her side; "we can't give out, all the time. We must stop occasionally to take something in, else our mental fuel runs low. I wonder if you realize that this is the one place in New York City where I can be entirely off my guard, entirely at home. A place like this means a good deal to an isolated man."

"I am very glad," she said quietly.

"Most people forget that a public singer has a private personality," he went on thoughtfully. "We are supposed to divide our time into even thirds, practising, singing and receiving compliments. It gets to be a positive delight to discuss the weather and the fashion in neckties."

"And to sing by the hour for your friends?" she inquired.

"It is our easiest way of speaking to them."

She laughed.

"But, on the other hand, you are demoralizing me completely. You have no idea what empty, formal affairs recitals seem to me now; they are so impersonal. I feel like grumbling, because I can't talk over each item of the programme with the one who does it. I said something of the sort to Miss Dane, the other day; but she told me she always dreaded the sound of a speaking voice after one of your songs."

"She might have a species of choral service evolved for social use," Thayer suggested dryly. "The Gregorian tones would lend dignity even to conventionalities, and they are quite within the powers of any amateur."

There was an interval of silence which Miss Gannion employed in bringing herself back to the physical world around her. Thayer's singing always swayed her profoundly; it gave her the impression of the ultimate satisfaction of a wish which had haunted her whole life. During the past two months, she and Thayer had established relations of cordial friendship. They had met frequently in the world which already was clamorous for Thayer's appearing, and Thayer was a frequent guest at Miss Gannion's home. He always sang to her; it had become so much a matter of routine that now he never waited for an invitation. Once seated at the piano, talking and singing by turns, she allowed him to follow out the bent of his mood; but, wherever it led him, she was always conscious of the insistent, throbbing note which told her that, underneath his self-control, there pulsed a fiery nature which was curbed, but not yet tamed, that the day might come when the Puritan would meet the Russian face to face, and the Russian would be dominant, if only for one brief hour. And then? Often as she asked herself the question, Margaret Gannion never swerved from her original answer. In the end, the Puritan would rule. No man could so dominate others and fail to dominate himself.

Thayer, meanwhile, had risen and was thoughtfully pacing the room. Miss Gannion shook off the last of her reverie and turned to watch him.

"What is it, Mr. Thayer?" she inquired suddenly.

He came back to the fire and, deliberately moving the trinkets on the mantel, made a place for his elbow. Then he hesitated, with his clear, deep-set eyes resting on her face.

"I think I am going to ask your advice," he said slowly.

"Or my approval. It amounts to the same thing in a man."

It was a direct challenge, and it was made with deliberate intention. Accustomed as she was to the semi-imaginary mental crises of struggling, strenuous youth, she yet shrank from the intentness of Thayer's mood.

He ignored the challenge.

"No; it is advice whether to act at all. Later, when I have acted, it will be time to demand your approval."

"But you may not like my advice."

"Very possibly. I am not binding myself to follow it."

Her color came again this time not altogether from pleasure.

"Then why do you ask it?"

"Because I need fresh light on the subject. As often as I go over it, I find myself in a mental blind alley, and I am hoping that, if I talk it over with you, I shall clear up my ideas and perhaps get some new ones."

His tone was dispassionate, yet kindly. With a pang, Miss Gannion admitted to herself the futility of her ever hoping to gain so impersonal an attitude. She was intensely feminine, which is to say, intensely subjective. Talking to Thayer in his present mood gave her the feeling that unexpectedly she had collided with an iceberg. Glittering coldness is an admirable surface to watch; but not an altogether comfortable one upon which to rest. The touch set her to stinging, although she realized that the sting was out of all proportion to the touch. She was silent, and Thayer went on,--

"You know the people, one of them much better than I do."

"Then it is not about yourself?"

Thayer shook his head.

"I rarely ask help in solving my own problems," he replied. Then, as he saw her face, he suddenly realized that he had hurt her in some unknown fashion. "That sounds rather brutal," he added; "but, if you will think it over a bit, you will see it is wise. I don't believe in wasting words, and there is no real use in talking some things over. A man knows he can't state his own problem impartially to someone else, so of course he isn't going to trust someone else's solution of the problem."

Her smile came back again.

"No," she assented; "but there is a certain comfort in talking things over."

"Not for me. If I have anything to do, I grit my teeth and do it, and waste as little thought upon it as possible. Iteration makes good into a bore. It is best to let it alone. And of bad, the less said, the better, that is, when it is a matter of one's own personality. But now I want to talk about Miss Dane."

"Beatrix?"

"Yes. I have felt anxious about her lately, and I haven't known whether to keep still, or to speak. It all seems a good deal like meddling, and I really know her so little."

It was unlike his usual directness to wander on in this fashion, and Miss Gannion wondered. She started to speak; then she thought better of it and leaned back in her chair. The ticking of the clock and the snapping of the fire mingled in a staccato duet. A stick burned in two and fell apart, with tiny, torch-like flames dancing on its upturned ends. Methodically Thayer bent over and piled up the embers. Then he spoke again.

"And so I thought I would speak to you about it. You have known Miss Dane always, and you know New York and how it looks at such things. I imagine you take it more seriously, here in America. It is serious, God knows, and yet it may not amount to anything."

Margaret Gannion straightened up and spoke with a sudden assumption of dignity which seemed to add inches to her moral and physical stature.

"To what are you referring, Mr. Thayer?"

"I beg your pardon. I thought you knew. I am talking about Lorimer."

"What about him?"

Man as he was, Thayer flinched under her keen eyes. All at once, he realized that Margaret Gannion included among her friends Beatrix Dane, and that it was Margaret Gannion's habit to fight for her friends.

"I had hoped you would understand without my putting it into so many words. Lorimer has been my friend for years, and it seems rather beastly to begin talking him over; but--"

"But?" Miss Gannion's tone was as hard and ringing as steel.

"But he sometimes takes a little more wine than is altogether wise," Thayer replied, with brief directness.

Miss Gannion dropped back in her chair.

"Does--does he get--drunk?" she questioned sharply.

"No. That is too strong a word. He is imprudent, foolish. Still, one never knows what may come."

"Poor Beatrix!" Miss Gannion said softly.

Thayer faced her again.

"Understand me, Miss Gannion; I am not doing this for love of gossip. Miss Dane is nothing to me, and I like Lorimer immensely. But there is a good deal at stake, and I am not sure how much I ought to leave to chance. Lorimer is one of the most lovable fellows in the world, generous and loyal; but he is weak. He was born so; I fancy it is in the blood. If Miss Dane is strong enough and has tact, perhaps she can hold him steady. He can't be driven an inch; but he can be led a long way."

Miss Gannion brushed her hair away from her face with an odd, bewildered gesture.

"Wait," she said breathlessly. "I love Beatrix, and it makes me slow to take this in. How long has it been going on?"

Thayer's lips tightened.

"Ever since I have known him," he answered reluctantly.

"Much?"

"No, comparatively little."

"Often?"

"Well--" The lengthening of the word told its own story.

"Does it increase?"

His expression answered her, and she took the answer in perfect silence. It was a full minute before she spoke again; but when she did speak, her voice had the old, level intonation.

"Are you willing to tell me just how far the trouble has gone, Mr. Thayer?"

"It is a hard matter to measure. Lorimer drinks less than a good many men; but it takes less to upset him. In Germany, the students all drink, and he was with them. As a rule, he stopped in time, but occasionally he was a little silly. Once or twice it was worse."

"How much worse?" The question was almost masculine in its direct brevity.

"I helped him to bed."

She compressed her lips. Then,--

"Go on," she said.

"I can't tell what happened while I was in Italy, and Lorimer had left Berlin before I went back there, so I didn't see him till I came to New York. At first, I thought he had stopped all that sort of thing. His color was better, his hand steadier. I knew the temptation was less here, and I hoped he was so taken up with Miss Dane that he wouldn't have time to get into the wrong set. The night of the Lloyd Avalons's recital, he was not quite himself, and I advised him to go to Washington while the matter blew over."

"Strange I didn't hear of it," Miss Gannion said thoughtfully.

"Dane and I saw to it that the story shouldn't get outside the walls of the smoking-room. Dane is a good fellow, and no fool. He got wind of the trouble and came for me, and we hurried Lorimer away as fast as possible. The next day, I began to hear of a supper or two where Lorimer had been making himself a bit conspicuous."

"And since then?"

"Only twice."

"But twice is more than enough."

"It shows that the trouble is still there, that one can't count on his promises," Thayer assented gravely.

"He does promise?"

"Yes, like a child. That is the pitiful part of it, pitiful and yet exasperating. He admits his own weakness, and is sorry and ashamed, as soon as he comes to himself. For a time, he is a model of caution and sobriety. Then he blunders into the way of temptation and makes a mess of it all." Unconsciously Thayer's voice betrayed his dislike of a weakness of which he had no comprehension. An instant later, he seemed to realize his own self-betrayal and he pulled himself up sharply. "I wish you knew Lorimer better, Miss Gannion. Then you would understand why I am telling you all this. He is so loyal, so generous to his friends, so full of talent. At Göttingen, they called him the most brilliant American who had ever studied there, and he was by all odds the most popular fellow of his time. His very popularity increased the danger." As if he had been pleading his own cause, Thayer's voice was full of earnest eagerness. Even in the midst of her anxiety and pain, Miss Gannion felt the power of its flexible modulation; and her half-formulated condemnation of Lorimer stayed itself.

Thayer broke the silence which followed, and his accent was resonant again.

"There's no especial use in thrashing over the past. The present is none too good; but my question is simply in relation to the future."

"And the question is?" Miss Gannion asked.

"Whether we ought to tell Miss Dane," he answered briefly.

"It will kill her." The feminine in Margaret Gannion was uppermost once more.

"Such wounds are more likely to mangle than to kill." Thayer spoke grimly.

"Poor Beatrix!"

"She does love him, then? I didn't see how she could help it."

Margaret Gannion's hands shut on a fold of her skirt.

"She loves him better than she loves her life; but she loves right better than either."

"And what is right?"

"I am not sure," she confessed weakly. "I can't seem to analyze it at all. What do you think?"

"That she ought to be told."

"What good will it do?"

"At least, it will put her on her guard."

"Against what? From your own showing, it is like fighting an unseen enemy. One never knows when or where it will come. She will only be put under a terrible nervous strain, faced by a fear that will haunt her, day and night. Besides, she might break the engagement. Have you thought of that?"

"It was of that I was thinking. She ought to have the facts, and be allowed to face the alternatives before it is too late. Miss Gannion," he turned upon her sharply; "can't you realize the pain it is to me to be saying this? I love Lorimer, love him as one man rarely loves another. Perhaps I love him all the more for his lack of strength. But that is no reason I should let him make havoc of a girl's whole life, perhaps of other lives to come. Miss Dane loves him; moreover, she is very proud. She is bound to suffer keenly on both scores."

"Then you think--"

"That the trouble is likely to increase."

"And, if she breaks her engagement to him?"

"That it will increase all the faster. She has a strong hold on him."

"And you would run the risk of loosing this hold, when you know the danger to your friend?"

"Yes, when I see the danger to Miss Dane."

Miss Gannion's hands unclasped, and she looked up at him with the pitiful, drooping lips of a frightened child. Like Thayer, she too loved Lorimer.

"It is terrible, Mr. Thayer. I can see no way out of the trouble; it stands on either side of the path. But do you think she could hold him, if she were to try?"

"It is an open question. Lorimer is weak; but I am not sure how strong she is, nor how patient. If she could steady him and forgive him ninety-nine times, it is possible that, on the hundredth, she would have nothing to forgive. But that is asking too much of a woman, that she should sacrifice her pride and her hope to her loyalty and her love."

"I think Beatrix would do it."

"Perhaps. At least, though, she ought to have the right to choose for herself."

Once more Miss Gannion mastered herself.

"I am not sure. You make the alternatives certain ruin and possible salvation. I should cling to the chance."

"And take the responsibility of silence?"

"It is a responsibility; but I should assume it for the present. What we should say to her could never be unsaid. It might do good; it might do terrible harm. It is possible that the truth may come to her in some other way. I should certainly prefer that it might."

He bent over the fire for a moment. Then he straightened up and threw back his shoulders, like a man relieved of the burden of a heavy load.

"Then that is your final advice?" he asked slowly.

She made answer just as slowly,--

"Mr. Thayer, I am growing older than I used to be, and things don't look quite so plain to me as they did once. Motives mix themselves more, and I am not so ready to put my finger on my neighbor's nerve. If I were in your place, I--rather think I should say my prayers, and then wait."

CHAPTER SEVEN

"I believe I should hate to have Mr. Thayer fall in love with me," Sally observed thoughtfully.

"I wouldn't worry about it yet," Bobby said unkindly. "He yawned twice, last night, while he was talking to you."

Sally's answer was prompt.

"Yes, we were discussing you."

"Why didn't you call me over to give you some points? It is the only subject upon which I can speak with authority. But just think what a lover Thayer would make, troubadouring around under windows!"

Sally counted swiftly.

"There are nineteen families in our hotel, Bobby, and thirteen of them have marriageable daughters. Imagine the creaking of casements, when Mr. Thayer warbled, 'Open the window to me, Love!' Troubadours will do for the country; in town, one can heed only the impersonal strains of the hurdy-gurdy. But really--"

"Yes?" Bobby's accent was encouraging.

"If Mr. Thayer should fall in love and get engaged, what could the girl call him? His name doesn't lend itself easily to endearments."

"His mother ought to have thought of that, when she named him."

"It is a case of visiting the father's sins upon the child of the sixth generation. He is only Volume Seven in the series of Cotton Mathers."

Bobby plunged his fists into his pockets.

"That is a respectable custom; but a mighty stupid one. A fellow oughtn't to be labelled like one of a class. Might as well catalogue children, and done with it, Alpha, Beta, Gamma, and so on through the list of Thayers. Then, when he came to years of discretion, he could pick for himself. Do you suppose I would have been Bobby, if I had been consulted?"

"What then?" Beatrix asked, pausing in her talk with Lorimer.

"Demosthenes Alphonso, of course. That's something worth while."

"Demosthenes Alphonso Dane. D. A. D." Sally commented irrepressibly. Then she swept across the room and, parting the curtains, peeped out between them. "Beatrix, the Philistines be upon you! Here comes Mrs. Lloyd Avalons. Oh, why was I the first to come? As a rule, I believe in the rotation of callers as implicitly as I do in the rotation of crops. Bobby, you came next. How long do you mean to stay?"

"Till the almonds are gone, or till Beatrix turns me out," he replied imperturbably.

"All right. Give me five minutes' warning. You can twirl your thumbs, when it is time for me to start; but I am bound to see some of the fun."

"Now, children, you must be good," Beatrix implored them hurriedly. "Bobby, do try to talk about something she can understand."

"If you want to condemn me to the conversational limits of a mummy, say so in plain Saxon," he retorted. "How can I talk about something that doesn't exist?"

"Bobby!" Sally's tone was full of warning, as Beatrix rose to meet her guest.

Mrs. Lloyd Avalons had gained one distinct point in her social training. She had learned to cross a room as if she were doing her hostess a favor by appearing. Even Beatrix was impressed by the swift, dainty sweep with which she came forward, and she cast a hasty thought to the quality of her tea. Bobby, meanwhile, was taking mental stock of Mrs. Lloyd Avalons's tailor and deciding that he could give points to his own fellow. For a person who professed to ignore all such detail, Bobby Dane was singularly critical of feminine dress, as Beatrix had learned to her cost.

Seated by the tea-table, balancing a Sèvres cup in her hand, Mrs. Lloyd Avalons appeared to be casting about in her mind for a subject of conversation. Bobby came to her relief.

"When you appeared, Mrs. Avalons, we were just speaking of mummies. Have you seen the latest importation at the Metropolitan?"

"Mr. Dane!" she remonstrated hastily. "Do you suppose I--"

"Certainly," Bobby assured her gravely. "I often spend an hour looking at them, and I always feel the better for the time passed in their society. They remind me of the futility of earthly things, and inspire me to higher aims."

Mrs. Lloyd Avalons smiled faintly.

"You literary people have strange thoughts," she observed, addressing the room at large. "I have often thought I should like to write, if I only had the time."

"Why don't you?" Bobby inquired blandly. "The result would be sure to be interesting."

But Beatrix interposed.

"Are you as busy as ever, Mrs. Avalons?"

"Busier. It is such a bore to be in this perpetual rush; but I can't seem to help it. Lent didn't bring me any rest, this year; and, now that Easter is over, it seems to me that we are more gay than ever."

"That is the penalty of having an early Easter," Sally suggested. "We had to stop for Lent in the middle of the season, and now we are finishing up the sins of which we have already repented."

"Oh--yes," Mrs. Lloyd Avalons responded blankly.

"Can you get all your arrears of penitence done up in six weeks, Sally?" Bobby asked, as he passed her the almonds.

"Yes, if I've not seen too much of you," she returned. "Mrs. Avalons, when are you going to give us another recital?"

Mrs. Lloyd Avalons rose to the cast.

"Wasn't that a success? Mr. Thayer quite covered himself with glory."

"His mantle fell over some of the rest of us, and we gained lustre from his glory." Sally's tone was slightly malicious.

"He is certainly a great artist, and I am proud to have discovered him."

"But I thought Mrs. Stanley discovered him. He sang for her first."

Mrs. Lloyd Avalons straightened in her chair. She had no intention of allowing to Mrs. Stanley the prestige which belonged to herself. Mrs. Stanley was several rounds farther up the social ladder than she was, herself; but Mrs. Stanley lacked initiative and was rapidly losing her start. In the seasons to come, she would find herself playing the part of understudy to Mrs. Lloyd Avalons.

"Oh, Mrs. Stanley heard he was to sing for me, and she cabled across to him to take an earlier steamer and sing for her first. It was a little tricky. What is it you call it in the business world, Mr. Dane?"

"A corner in Cotton," Bobby replied gravely.

Mrs. Lloyd Avalons thought she could see that the point of this joke was directed against Mrs. Stanley, and she laughed rather more heartily than good breeding required. In her mirth, she even bent forward in her chair, writhing slightly to and fro, while her silken linings hissed like angry snakes. Suddenly she realized that she had prolonged her mirth beyond the limits of the others, and she straightened her face abruptly.

"But I am so glad the subject has come up, Miss Dane," she went on. "I was meaning to ask you whether you thought I could get Mr. Thayer to sing for our Fresh Air Fund."

"Really, I have no idea of Mr. Thayer's engagements," Beatrix said drily.

"But I thought you knew him so well."

Beatrix's face expressed her surprise.

"I know him as I know any number of people, Mrs. Avalons. That doesn't mean that Mr. Thayer consults me in regard to his plans."

"Oh, no," Mrs. Lloyd Avalons responded vivaciously. "But couldn't you just say a good word for us?"

"I am afraid it wouldn't count for much."

Mrs. Lloyd Avalons raised her brows and made a delicate, pushing gesture with her outspread palms.

"You are too modest, Miss Dane. We all know your powers of persuasion, and we are counting on you."

"Who are *we*?" Sally inquired, in flat curiosity.

"Mrs. Van Bleeker and Mrs. Knickerbocker and I. We are the committee, this year, and we are trying to have an uncommonly good concert."

"It must be very hard for you to work on a music committee with Mrs. Van Bleeker," Bobby suggested. "She doesn't know a fugue from a bass viol, and she never hesitates to say so."

"Therein she differs from most unmusical people," Sally responded, in a swift aside. "Even truthful people will fib valiantly, where music is concerned, and go into raptures, when they have hard work to suppress their yawns. It was a sorry day for music, when it became the fashion."

"How droll you are, Miss Van Osdel!" Mrs. Lloyd Avalons was nothing, if not direct, in her personal comments. Then she answered Bobby. "Even if Mrs. Van Bleeker isn't really musical, it is a delight to work with her, she is so very charming and so business-like. Strange as it may seem, I actually take pleasure in our committee meetings, Mr. Dane."

"I haven't the slightest doubt of it," Bobby responded, with unctuous emphasis.

"When is the concert to be, Mrs. Avalons?" Beatrix asked hastily, with a frown at her cousin who stared blandly back at her.

"The first week in May, if we can possibly be ready for it. There was so much, just before Lent, that we postponed it until after Easter. Now we are no better off, for every day is full, so we are delaying it again. We want to make it a large affair, don't you know, something that will attract the swell set and the musical people, too."

If Bobby Dane hated one word in the language, that word was *swell*. Accordingly, he glared haughtily across the table at Mrs. Lloyd Avalons, noting, as he did so, the scornful cadence of her voice over the final phrase.

"The two sets rarely mingle, Mrs. Avalons. Which is under your especial care?"

Lorimer interposed hurriedly, for he felt the hostility in Bobby's tone, and he was ignorant of the thickness of Mrs. Lloyd Avalons's skin.

"Both, I should say from the make-up of your recital, Mrs. Avalons. Society and art both spelled themselves with capital letters, that night."

"I am sure it is very kind of you to say so," she answered, while her pleasure brought the first sincere note into her voice. "I tried to have something really good. But about this concert; we are to have a soprano from the Metropolitan Opera House, and possibly a violinist, and we want Mr. Thayer so much. Do you suppose we could get him?"

"It might depend a little upon the state of your finances," Bobby suggested.

"Oh; but it is for charity, you know."

"Yes, charity is supposed to be like molasses, sweet and cheap. It isn't very nourishing to a professional man, though."

"But Mr. Thayer is not poor."

"That doesn't signify that he can give all his time for nothing," Bobby answered rather warmly, considering that the question was utterly impersonal. "If he sang every day, all winter, for some charity or other, he couldn't begin to get round in ten years. There ought to be a new mission started, a Society for the Protection of Over-begged Artists."

"But I am only asking him for one charity."

"That's all anybody is supposed to do. The time hasn't come yet when you syndicate the job, though I suppose it is only a matter of time."

Mrs. Lloyd Avalons looked at him distrustfully for a moment; then she laughed with a dainty vagueness.

"You are so amusing, Mr. Dane! One never really knows whether you're in earnest or not. How many tickets did you say you would take?"

"One and a half," Sally advised, while Bobby stared at Mrs. Lloyd Avalons in speechless disgust. "He will go, and take me with him; but newspaper men are always admitted at half-rates."

"And you really think Mr. Thayer will sing for us?" Mrs. Lloyd Avalons went on, turning back to Beatrix. "It will be an advantage to him, in a way, to have sung under the auspices of our committee."

This time, even Beatrix felt herself antagonized. Thayer belonged to her own class, and her class was scarcely of the type to need the official social sanction of Mrs. Lloyd Avalons.

"I have no idea at all in regard to the matter," she answered a little coldly. "Mr. Thayer appears to me to be able to hold his own, without the backing of any committee. It simply depends upon his personal generosity."

"But it is such a worthy object. And don't you think we could get that little Arlt to fill in with?"

"From, by, in, or with charity, and to or for a charity?" Bobby asked savagely.

"Oh, of course, we couldn't pay him." There was a falling inflection of the last word.

"Then I should advise him to decline charity altogether," Bobby retorted.

"It would be an advantage to him to play on such a programme," Mrs. Lloyd Avalons asserted, as she set down her cup.

"It would also be an advantage to him to get a little money, now and then."

Mrs. Lloyd Avalons raised her brows. They were daintily-marked brows, and the expression suited her pretty, empty little face.

"I think it is something for a man of no reputation at all to have a chance to be heard in such a connection," she replied a little tartly.

"Ye-es." Bobby rose with provoking deliberation. "And it is also possible, Mrs. Avalons, that when we are thankful even to be charted in Woodlawn, Mr. Arlt's name may be a good deal better known than it is now. Sally, we are due at the Stuyvesants', and I think we must tear ourselves away."

Out in the hall, he addressed himself to Sally.

"For social pulleys, give me three: music, cheek, and charity, but the greatest of these is ch--"

"Charity," amended Sally promptly.

Bobby gloomily pulled himself into his overcoat.

"Sally, I abhor that woman," he said.

CHAPTER EIGHT

"If you once begin, there'll be no end to it," Bobby warned Thayer, when he announced his intention of singing for the Fresh Air Fund.

"I never yet found anything I couldn't end, when I tried," Thayer returned coolly.

Bobby eyed him askance.

"Ever tackled Mrs. Lloyd Avalons's idiocy?" he queried.

"She is not the only one."

"No; worse luck! But what makes you do it?"

"I approve the charity, and I happened to have a free night. Moreover, it will give Arlt a chance to accompany."

"But she won't pay him."

"No, but I generally manage to pay my own accompanist."

"Do you think he will gain from such a thing?"

Crossing his knees comfortably, Thayer lighted the pipe he had been filling, and took a tentative puff or two.

"I don't know," he said dubiously. "He ought to, but I can't seem to discover the way to get on in this precious country of ours. Arlt is a musician to the tips of his fingers; I have yet to hear a pianist in the city to compare with him. And still, nobody manifests the least interest in him."

Bobby contemplated the tip of his own cigar, bending his brows and frowning as much from his optical angle as from his mental one.

"He lacks the two P's," he said slowly; "pull and personality."

Impatiently Thayer uncrossed his knees and crossed them in the reverse position.

"Do you mean that nothing else counts here?" he demanded.

"Precious little. A fellow has got to have good lungs for blowing his own horn, else he is drowned in the general chorus. That's the worst of music as a profession; personality is everything. You must be perfect or peculiar. The latter alternative is the greater help. If Arlt would grow a head of hair, or wear a dinner napkin instead of a necktie, it would improve his chances wonderfully."

"But, if the right people would take him up?" Thayer suggested.

"They won't; or, if they do, they'll drop him as a monkey drops a hot chestnut. Arlt plays like an artist; but he blushes, and he forgets to keep his cuffs in sight. He is as unworldly as he is conventional. Society doesn't care to fuss with him."

Thayer looked grave.

"I am having my own share of good times, Dane. It seems as if I ought to be able--"

Bobby interrupted him.

"You can't. No man can hoist his brother into success. It is bound to be every man for himself. You can work over Arlt till the crack of doom, and that's all the good it will do him. People will say 'How noble of Mr. Thayer!' and they will burn moral tapers about your feet; and meanwhile they'll leave Arlt sitting on the floor alone in the dark."

"Nevertheless, I think I shall keep on with the experiment," Thayer said stubbornly.

"Good luck go with you! But it won't. You can't make the next man's reputation; he must do it for himself. All art is bound to be a bit selfish; but music is the worst of the lot. I don't mean composing, of course, but the interpreting end of it. It's such beastly personal work; all the nooks and corners of your individuality show up across the footlights. They are commented upon, and they have to pass muster. Artistically, you and Arlt are as alike as two peas; personally, you are positive, he is negative.'"

There was a pause. Then Thayer said quietly,--"I think I shall sing the Damrosch *Danny Deever*. It has a stunning accompaniment."

The committee of the Fresh Air Fund concert showed themselves a potent trio, and their concert became recognized as the official finale of the musical season. Their meetings had been fraught with interest, for time, place and programme all came under detailed discussion. It must be at a time neither too soon after Easter to collide with it, nor too late to have a place in the season's gayety. The place must be lofty enough to lure the world of fashion; yet not so lofty as to deter the simpler folk to whom the white and gold of the Waldorf ballroom was a mere name, as remote from their lives as the *Petit Trianon*. The programme must be classic enough to satisfy the critic; yet tuneful enough not to bore the amateur, and accordingly it roamed from Brahms to Molloy, and included that first Slavonic Dance of Dvorák which sets the pulses of Pagan and Philistine alike to tingling with a barbarous joy in the mere consciousness of living. Thayer alone had refused to accept dictation at the hands of the committee.

"If I consent to sing, I must choose my own songs," he had said quietly to Mrs. Lloyd Avalons, when she had suggested a modern French love song in place of the Händel aria he had selected.

"Oh, but it is so late in the season, and everybody is tired," she had urged gayly. "If we give them too heavy things on a warm night, they may go to sleep."

"Then I shall proceed to wake them up," he replied. "And, for the second number, the *Danny Deever*, I think."

"Mr. Thayer! That grewsome thing! Why don't you sing *My Desire*, if you are so anxious for an American song?"

"I think *Danny* will be better. Then we will consider it settled." And it was not until she was out on the stairs that Mrs. Lloyd Avalons realized she had been defeated and then dismissed by the man whose patroness she was assuming to be.

"No matter," she reflected; "we've got to pay Signora Cantabella, and we can insist upon her singing something a little more digestible. Mr. Thayer is cranky; but we get him and that little Arlt for nothing, so I suppose we mustn't be too critical."

For once, Mrs. Lloyd Avalons showed her good sense. In all truth, beggars should not be choosers, whether the alms be of bread crusts or of high art.

Lorimer dined with Beatrix, that night. Contrary to the custom of the Danes, they did not linger over the meal; and, as soon as they left the table, Beatrix and Lorimer strolled away to the conservatory at the back of the house. The yellow sunset light was still gilding the place, and through the wide-open windows the night breeze crept in, softly stirring the heavy palm leaves and scattering the scent of a few late violets over all the air.

Refusing the seat which Lorimer silently pointed out to her, Beatrix paced restlessly up and down the broad middle walk.

"I think I am nervous, to-night," she said, with an odd little laugh. "I have been feeling, all day long, as if things were going to happen."

"Things generally do happen," Lorimer said lightly, as he sauntered along by her side.

"Yes; but something unusual, something uncanny."

Lorimer threw back his head and laughed.

"I thought you derided presentiments, Beatrix."

She bit her lip.

"I do," she said, after a pause. "I know it is foolish, and I am ashamed of myself; but I dread this recital, to-night, and I dread that hateful Lloyd Avalons supper after it. Let's not go, Sidney."

"Oh, but we must. Why not?"

"They are such impossible people."

"I know; but everyone will understand that it is on Thayer's account that we go, Beatrix. And he made such a point of it."

She drew a long breath.

"If we must--But I dread it. Do keep Mr. Avalons away from me, then."

As he looked down at the brown head which scarcely rose above his lips, Lorimer's smile ceased to be whimsical and became inexpressibly tender and winning.

"Count on me, dear girl. He is a brute; but I won't let him go near you."

Impulsively she turned and faced him.

"Sidney," she said, with a breathless catch in her voice; "Sidney--" Then, while she hesitated, she raised her hands and rested them on his broad shoulders. "Sidney dearest, do you know what it is to love as I love you? It would kill me to have anything come in between us."

Startled by her overwrought nerves, he put his arm around her and drew her head against his shoulder.

"I know only one thing, Beatrix," he said gravely; "nothing now can come between us but death."

Diamond aigrettes and critical ears both were at the concert, that night, mingled with a fair sprinkling of those to whom the charity appealed far more than did the mere musical and worldly phases of the affair. The little folded programmes were in a way typical of the whole situation: one page containing the modest announcement of the Fresh Air Fund concert, the next one the simple statement of the numbers of the programme, while the third, in full-faced type bore the majestic list of patronesses. Between his German and Italian fellow artists and his polysyllabic Dutch sponsors, Thayer's name stood out in all the aggressiveness of Puritan simplicity.

As a whole, the concert was as frothy as was the audience. The songs glittered like the diamonds, and the orchestra played the *Valkyries' Ride* with a cheerful abandonment of mirth.

"Thayer is the only dignified member of the company," Bobby growled into Sally's ears, as the last note of his aria died away. "The rest of them are doing tricks like a set of vaudeville artists. I expected that violinist to play cadenzas with his violin held in the air above his head. You don't catch Thayer dropping into such trick work."

"He doesn't need to; he can 'scorn such a foe' to his heart's content, for he is getting the applause of the evening. Does he sing again?"

"The very last number. It is an unusual place, to wind up a programme after the orchestra is through; but I think he is equal to it."

Beatrix felt every nerve in her body tingling and throbbing, when Thayer came out on the stage for the second time. As a whole, the concert had not been inspiring to her; it had been too obviously popular. Yet, at least, it had tended to relax her strained nerves. Gade concertos are a species of mental gruel, easy to assimilate and none too stimulating; but all the innate barbarism of humanity, all of her nervous force responded to the clashing rhythm of the Slavonic Dance, and the swift color came into her face and focussed itself in a tiny circle in either cheek, as she listened. For the moment, she was as fiercely defiant of fate as a Valkyrie flying forth to battle.

The mood was still upon her, as Thayer came striding out across the stage. Arlt was beside him, for Thayer had refused an orchestral accompaniment and had left *Danny Deever* in the hands of a pianist. His choice had been a wise one for Arlt. The two of them had spent hours over the song, and the young German surpassed himself in the swift changes of *motif* until, as he left *Danny's* soul freeing itself from the swinging body and took up the cheery theme of the quickstep once more, even Thayer was relegated momentarily to the background, as a mere librettist to the passionate fury of the accompaniment.

Again and again the applause broke out; again and again Thayer insisted upon leading Arlt before the audience to make his bow; but still the audience refused to be satisfied. Even the most graceful of bows is not enough, when one is thoroughly aroused.

"Play something, Arlt," Thayer ordered him at last.

Arlt shook his head.

"It is for you they are calling."

"Nonsense. This is your success; not mine."

Arlt demurred; but in the end he yielded and played one or two numbers of Schumann's *Papillon*, played them like a true artist. As he listened, Thayer held his breath. At last, Arlt's chance had come, and he was making the most of it. The furore of a moment before had been for Arlt more than for himself. Sad experience had taught him the futility of *Danny*, unless it were adequately accompanied, and the audience were discerning enough to give honor to whom honor was due. Standing in the wings, Thayer exulted in each note which fell from the boy's fingers, round and mellow and weighted with passionate meaning. Arlt was betraying his hopes and fears more than he realized, just then, and Thayer grew impatient for his closing phrase, that he might hear the storm of applause which was bound to follow. He had not counted upon the veering wind of popular interest which scattered the storm, leaving only the gentle patter of a summer shower. The critics applauded; but society applied its lorgnette to its eye and discovered that, in his excitement, Arlt had neglected to make sure that his tie was mathematically straight. The patter died away into silence. Then the wind veered again and the storm broke out afresh, mingled with cries of Thayer's name.

Arlt's lips worked nervously, as he joined Thayer in the wings.

"It was you they wanted, after all," he said, with a pitiful attempt at a smile.

"Then they are damned fools," Thayer replied savagely; but his hand was gentle, as he rested it on Arlt's shoulder.

The boy braced himself at the touch.

"We must go back," he said.

Thayer hesitated, while his thoughts worked swiftly. There would be a certain cruelty, to his mind, in forcing Arlt to appear again before the audience which had just cut him so mercilessly. On the other hand, it would be the part of childish pique for him to refuse to show himself. Nevertheless, he needed Arlt's support. He disliked to play his own accompaniments, and he felt that, in doing so, he risked possible disaster. The hesitation lasted only for a moment. Then his jaw stiffened.

"It's all right, Arlt," he said briefly. "I am going to accompany myself, this time."

As he crossed the stage, he glanced hastily from Bobby to Bobby's cousin. Bobby was glowering at the audience and grumbling into Sally's ear. Four rows in front of them, Beatrix sat silent at Lorimer's side. The color had left her face again, and her eyes drooped heavily. It was as if, in watching Arlt's overthrow, her old prescience of impending disaster had come back upon her in fourfold measure, heightened by the intensity of her exhilaration of a few moments before. When a quiet woman is stirred from her usual poise, the pendulum of her nerves swings in a long arc. The Dvorák dance had not deepened Sally's color; the Damrosch song had not caused her to draw her white ostrich boa more closely about her throat.

Thayer struck a vigorous major chord or two; then, with a sudden memory of the dry glitter in Arlt's eyes, he modulated thoughtfully. His own eyes rested again upon Beatrix during the few notes of the introduction, and his mind went swiftly back to the day when he had sung the same little song in her parlor.

Half absently, his eyes were still upon her face, as he came again to the closing words,--

"I kiss each bead, and strive at last to learn To kiss the cross, sweetheart, to kiss the cross."

Unconsciously, uncontrollably, his eyes held hers, and he could see the two great drops gather there, as she listened, her lips parted with her deep, swift breathing. Then their eyes dropped apart, and the color rushed into her cheeks while, with a sudden, impulsive gesture, she slipped her hand into Lorimer's arm and pressed it until she felt the returning, reassuring pressure.

Lorimer looked down at her with a smile.

"Spooky again, dear girl?" he asked, under cover of the applause which had broken out madly once more. "He is singing superbly, to-night; but this last was wonderful. Something has rubbed him the wrong way; I know that set of his jaw, and it always means that he will be inspired to do his best. Queer thing; isn't it? If I were angry or hurt, I should go to pieces completely; but it brings Thayer to his feet, every time."

"What do you think was the reason?" Beatrix asked, with as great a show of interest as she could command. The first lesson Mrs. Dane had taught her child in preparation for her coming-out tea had been the simple and obvious one that men were rarely minded to sympathize with feminine moods; but that under all conditions a woman who seeks to please, must adapt herself to the mental vagaries of her masculine companion. Even Lorimer, tender and loving as he invariably showed himself, was no exception to the rule.

"It was Arlt's snubbing," Lorimer returned, as he rose. "It was a beastly thing to do. Arlt played superbly, and they might have treated him with common courtesy. But there is no accounting for tastes. Thayer is the hero of the evening, and people are too busy applauding him, to have any time for lesser lights."

"Do you think Mr. Arlt will ever succeed?" she asked anxiously for, through Thayer's efforts to bring them together, she had become genuinely interested in the boy.

"God knows," Lorimer answered, with a sudden gravity that became him well.

Later, that evening, Thayer joined Lorimer and Beatrix in a corner of the Lloyd Avalons's music-room. Beatrix greeted him half shyly.

"It was a new experience," she said, with an effort to speak lightly. "I thought I had learned to know your voice long ago; but I have decided that I never really knew it, until to-night."

He stood looking down at her with a grave smile.

"My voice isn't always reliable, Miss Dane. Once in a while, it seems to run away with me. To-night, it took the bits in its teeth."

She felt compelled to raise her eyes to meet his.

"I hope it won't do it too often. It is wonderful; but--" Then she pulled herself together with a little laugh. "It must be rather amusing to you, Mr. Thayer, to watch your effect on your audience, and to know that you can make them shiver or cry whenever you choose."

He refused to be won into the laugh for which she hoped.

"It isn't whenever I choose," he responded, with unexpected literalness. "Sometimes I feel as if I were the victim of a sort of possession. I believe I have a demon that inhabits my vocal cords upon occasion. If he does get hold of me, I am merely a machine in his hands. When I become my own manager again, I am never quite sure what I may have been doing."

"Something very good, to-night. But where is Mr. Arlt?"

Thayer's face darkened.

"Mrs. Lloyd Avalons neglected to invite him," he replied quietly.

Lorimer's lip curled.

"If that isn't beyond the dreams of snobbishness, Thayer! Why did you come to her old party, then?"

"Because I thought it would be too petty to stay away."

"I would be petty, then. But, as far as that goes, Arlt's ancestors were gentlemen, when hers were shovelling gravel for a dollar a day. American democracy runs in strange grooves. Thayer, I am going to leave Beatrix in your care for a few minutes. I promised Ned Carpenter I would see him in the smoking-room, to make a date for his yachting cruise."

Thayer looked after him with a certain anxiety which clouded his gray eyes and found a reflection in the face of his companion. The cloud remained, although their talk went on as if nothing were amiss. In fact, nothing was amiss; it was only that their nerves, jarred by Arlt's failure, were looking for disaster upon every hand. For the time being, each bead seemed tipped with its cross. Both felt it; both were loath to acknowledge the feeling by so much as a look.

Suddenly Thayer roused himself.

"Lorimer has been detained, Miss Dane, and we both are growing hungry. May I take you to the dining-room?"

Side by side, they crossed the floor, now almost deserted, and reached the door of the dining-room whence came a confused noise of buzzing tongues and clattering dishes. Then, above all else, Lorimer's voice met their ears, a merry, laughing voice, but strangely thick as regarded its consonants.

"An' so, 's I was shayin', we wen' to Mory's, one ni', an' there was thish man--"

Some unaccountable impulse made him raise his eyes just then. They fell full upon Beatrix standing in the doorway, with Thayer at her side.

CHAPTER NINE

Beatrix's library was full of women, when Lorimer put in a tardy appearance, the day after the Fresh Air Fund concert. A dozen little tables littered with cards were pushed together in one corner, and the tinkling of china and the hum of conversation betrayed the fact that whist had given place to a more congenial method of passing the time. Modern womanhood plays whist almost without ceasing; but it should be noted that she frowns over the whist and reserves her smiles for her more garrulous interludes.

Lorimer, as he stepped across the threshold, felt a sudden longing to retreat. He had forgotten both the whist and the interlude, that afternoon, and he felt no inclination to exchange verbal inanities with a group of women of whom several had been at the Lloyd Avalons supper, the night before. All of them, he was convinced, had heard of the incident, and were covertly eying Beatrix to see whether she looked as if she had slept well. His theory was justified by the fact that, for the first time that season, not a substitute had been present.

Beatrix rose from the tea table, as he crossed the room towards her. Her manner was a shade more alert than usual; but her eyes, half-circled in heavy shadows, drooped before his eyes, as she gave him her hand. He felt her fingers shake a little, and he could see the color die out of her cheeks. Otherwise, there was nothing to mark their meeting as in any way differing from any other meeting in the past. He greeted the other women, accepted his cup of tea and took up his share of the burden of conversation with apparent nonchalance.

The nonchalance was only apparent, however. Lorimer had sought Beatrix, that day, much in the mood in which the naughty boy turns his back to receive his allotted caning. The bad half-hour was bound to come; it was best to have it over as soon as possible. Lorimer had gone to bed, the night before, in a state of maudlin cheeriness. He had wakened, that morning, feeling a heavy weight in his head and a heavier one on his conscience. He had an unnecessarily clear recollection of Beatrix's face as it had looked to him, the one sharply-outlined fact across a misty distance peopled with vague shadows. The eyes had been hurt and angry; but the lips showed only loving disappointment. All the morning long, he had pondered upon the matter; but by noon he had made his decision. The meeting was inevitable, so what was the use of trying to put it off?

"Well, Sidney?" Beatrix said steadily, as soon as the last guest had made her nervous, chattering exit.

With some degree of care, he had prepared his defensive argument; but it had lost all its force and fervor by reason of the half-hour spent in the roomful of women. Now he made a hasty effort to reconstruct it, and failed.

"I am sorry," he said, with simple humility.

Unconsciously, each had taken the best method to disarm the other. Before scornful, angry denunciation, he could have burst out into voluble explanation and defence which, in its turn, would have antagonized Beatrix beyond any possibility of relenting. For the unpardonable sin, forgiveness must be a free gift. Confronted by excuses, Beatrix would have been unyielding. In the face of his humility, she hesitated to speak the final condemnation, and instinct taught her that feminine reproaches were worse than futile in the face of a real crisis.

[Illustration: "'Can't you make any sort of an excuse for yourself, Sidney?' she demanded"]

"How did you happen to do it, Sidney?" she asked quietly, as she seated herself again beside the deserted tea table and began absently setting the disordered cups into straight rows.

He raised his eyes from the carpet.

"Because I was a brute," he said briefly.

Methodically she sorted out the spoons in two little piles. Then, pushing them together into a disorderly heap, she started to her feet and faced him.

"Can't you make any sort of an excuse for yourself, Sidney?" she demanded, and there was a desperate ring to her words.

He shook his head.

"I can't see any," he replied, after an interval. Suddenly he laughed harshly. "Unless you count total depravity," he added.

She ignored the laugh.

"I suppose you know, then, what this means," she said slowly, so slowly that it seemed as if each word caught in her throat.

His face whitened and he started to speak; but his voice failed him. He bowed in silence.

"I am sorry," she went on, while the cords in her clasped hands stood out like bits of rattan; "perhaps I am more sorry than you are; but there seems to be nothing else that I can do. Last night was the tragedy of my life; to-day is the hardest, the longest day I have ever spent. But--"

Bending forward, he took up one of the spoons from the table and looked at it intently for a moment. Under his mustache his lips worked nervously, and Beatrix saw the moisture gather in great drops upon his forehead. Fortunately she could not see his eyes, for their long lashes veiled them. It was better so; she could hold herself more steady. There was a certain mercilessness in the way she waited for him to break the silence.

"Is it final?" he asked at length. "I wish you would give me another chance, Beatrix."

"I have given you too many, as it is," she replied sadly.

He looked up at her, too much startled now to care whether or not she saw the tell-tale tears.

"How do you mean?"

"That last night only confirmed what I have been suspecting and dreading." This time, there came the scornful note he had so feared.

He dropped his eyes again, and accepted the condemnation in silence. If she knew the whole truth, there was no need of arguing with her over the details. The spoon snapped in two in his hands. He rose and tossed the fragments into the fire.

"Where are you going?" Beatrix asked.

"Straight to the devil." His accent was hard, but perfectly quiet, the accent of a desperate man, not of a reckless boy.

Up to the last moment, she had expected that he would seek to justify himself, would ask her to explain her decision and to modify it. This grim, silent acceptance of his fate terrified her. It seemed to throw upon her shoulders all the responsibility of an action which in itself was right, yet possibly burdened with consequences dangerous to another. For herself, for the killing of her own great love, Beatrix never wavered. It was her own affair and concerned herself alone. But she knew that Lorimer loved her, and all at once she realized that her sudden rejection of his love was bound to bring forth bitter fruit. During the time it took him to cross the floor, she was swiftly weighing her duty to herself against her duty to her neighbor. She was bound to send him away; but was she equally bound to send him away like a beaten dog, without a word of explanation or of pity?

"Sidney?"

He had reached the door; but, at her call, he hesitated and looked back.

"You understand why I am doing this?"

"Yes," he said bitterly; "I understand only too well."

"And you think I am justified?"

He faced about squarely.

"Good God, Beatrix, when you have stabbed a man to death, don't grind the knife round and round, and ask him if he feels it! Let him make as plucky an exit as he can."

His words broke the strain she had put upon herself.

"I didn't mean--I didn't suppose--" she faltered. Then she dropped into a chair and covered her face with her hands.

Lorimer turned to the door again, halted irresolutely, then went back to her side.

"I can't go away and leave you like this, dear girl," he said, as he bent over her. "It isn't going to be easy for either of us; it is bound to leave a terrible scar on our lives. But, if it is the only thing you can do: at least, can't we say a decent good-by to each other?"

She took down her hands, drew a long breath and looked up at him; but she was unable to meet the look in his eyes, the loving, hungry look which she had learned to know so well.

"We have loved each other, dear girl. I have been better and stronger for your love. I only wish it might have lasted, for in time it might have made me quite steady. But I am glad I have had so much. Whatever the future has for me, at least I have had something in the past."

The hardness had left his tone, and the passionate, bitter ring. There was nothing now but the note of utter sadness. Beatrix trembled for herself, for the fate of her resolve, as she heard it.

"But I couldn't hold you, Sidney."

"No, dear; perhaps not. But you held me more than you knew. You only saw the times I slipped; you never had any idea of the times I nearly went under, and pulled myself up again for your sake. If it hadn't been for you and Thayer, for Thayer before I ever saw you, dear, I should have gone under long ago. Now Thayer will have it all to do."

There was no reproach in his voice. He seemed to be merely stating the fact, not entirely for her ears, but as if he were trying to accustom himself to the thought of all which it implied. Suddenly his shoulders straightened; his tone grew resonant; his words came more rapidly.

"It is in my blood, Beatrix. My mother was weak, and I am weaker still. I know the danger; I see it and I tell myself that I must fight shy of it. For a while I do fight shy of it, till I get off my guard and think I am quite safe. The next thing I know, it has cropped out again, and I haven't the nerve to face it and knock it over. It knocks me over, instead, and each knock is just a little harder than the one before it has been. I realize it, and I try to down it; but that's all the good it does. I am weak, Beatrix, weak and selfish. I honestly think it is harder for me to keep steady than it would be for Thayer, or even for Bobby. The taint is in me. I don't mean that it is any excuse for my making a brute of myself; but, if there is any pity in God, he must give a little bit of it to us fellows, born weak, realizing our weakness and truly meaning to fight it, and yet giving in to it again and again."

"There is pity in God, Sidney," she said drearily; "but pity can't do any good in a case like this. You need help, not pity."

"The help of man?" he asked bitterly. "Who will give it? They are too busy saving themselves."

"There is only one man who can help you."

"Thayer?"

"No; yourself. Sidney, I hate to discuss this thing, for it has come between us and spoiled life for us both; but you have no right to depend on Mr. Thayer as you do. You aren't a child, and you can fight your own way out of this."

"What's the use now?"

"Use! Everything. Your whole manhood."

"But in the end? What does it all amount to?"

"Surely, you aren't child enough to need a bribe?" she asked in sharp scorn.

Her scorn stung him to rapid speech.

"Beatrix, ever since I turned into manhood, I have known this danger of mine, and I have tried to fight it for the sake of the woman I might love, some day. Laugh, if you will. Perhaps it is funny; but it has a certain pitiful side to it, this trying to keep one's self clean for the sake of the woman one has never yet seen. Then, last fall, I did see her. Since then, the fight has been easier; perhaps I've not lost so many battles. It all seemed more worth while. And now--"

"And now?" Her voice was almost inaudible.

"Now I have had it all and lost it, lost it through my own fault, and there doesn't seem to be anything left worth fighting for."

There was a long silence. At length, Beatrix rose.

"Sidney," she said, as she slowly held out both hands to him; "shall we fight side by side for a little longer?"

CHAPTER TEN

"I've manufactured a new definition of happiness," Sally said to Bobby Dane, six months later.

"What now?"

"Think with the mob."

"Who has rubbed you the wrong way, this time?" Bobby queried unsympathetically.

"Everybody. I am so tired of hearing people praise Beatrix for marrying Sidney Lorimer."

Bobby halted and shook hands with her, to the manifest wonder of the post-ecclesiastical Fifth Avenue throng.

"That's where even your head is level, Sally," he said, as he resumed his stroll. "Do you want to know what I think of her?"

"If you agree with me; not otherwise. I hate arguments, and, besides, it is bad form to condemn one's dearest friend. But keeping still so long has nearly driven me to--"

"Tetanus," Bobby suggested. "Well, my impression of Beatrix is that she is a bally idiot. I don't know just what *bally* means; but our English brethren apply it in critical cases, and so it is sure to be right. Yes, I think Beatrix is very bally indeed."

"Then you don't approve, either?"

"Me? I? I have hated Lorimer from the start."

"I haven't," Sally said, after a thoughtful interval. "I liked him at first."

"You never saw him at the club," Bobby returned briefly.

"What did he do there?"

"I don't know. He just wasn't right."

Sally paced along meditatively at his side.

"Bobby, you are a critical being," she observed at length.

"Mayhap. But the event justifies me. I never have liked Lorimer, and I never shall."

"What are you going to do about it?"

Bobby opened his hands and turned them palm downwards.

"There's nothing to be done. I hate to see Beatrix throw herself away; but I can't help it."

"I wonder what her idea is," Sally said thoughtfully. "She has always been so down upon any fastness that I supposed she would cut his acquaintance entirely, after that Lloyd Avalons supper."

"He acted an awful cad, that night." Bobby's tone was disdainful. "I helped get him home and, before he was fairly out of the dining-room, he was bragging about his family, and his money, and the Lord knows what."

"Yes, I heard him. Beatrix heard some of it, too, before Mr. Thayer took her away. I was at her house, the next afternoon, when Mr. Lorimer called, and I was sure she would break her engagement there and then. Put not your faith in the principles of a woman in love."

"Confound her principles! That's what is the matter with her," Bobby growled. "I had always supposed that Beatrix was a reasonable girl; but no girl in her senses would tackle the job of marrying Sidney Lorimer to reform him."

"When I do it, I'll reverse things and reform the man to marry him," Sally returned shrewdly.

Bobby raised his brows.

"The first time you've ever warned me that I was on probation, Sally!"

"I said a man, not a boy," she replied unkindly. "But, after all, Mr. Lorimer has been perfectly steady, all summer long."

"Mm--yes, after a fashion. Of course, he would do his best, for I will do him the justice to admit that he loves Beatrix with all the manhood there is in him. To be sure, that's not saying much."

"You aren't quite fair to him, Bobby. He must have some manhood in him, to have steadied down as much as he has done, this summer."

Bobby shrugged his shoulders.

"He is playing for high stakes, Sally, and he can afford to be careful. Any slip now would prove to be the losing of the whole game. Wait a year and see."

"Then you think--"

"That his reform is skin deep, and that, like all other serpents, he sloughs his skin once a year."

"Bobby!"

"Sarah Maria!"

"Don't make fun of me because I was named for a spinster aunt. I can't help my name."

"No; it's past help. I'd change it, if I were you. Just think how it would sound at the altar, while the alteration was going on! 'I, Sarah Maria, take thee--'"

Sally interposed hurriedly.

"But, to go back to Beatrix, if you feel in this way about Mr. Lorimer, why don't you do something about it?"

"Do what, for example?"

"Speak to her father, or something."

Bobby's answer had an accent of utter gravity which somehow belied the frivolous form of his words.

"Sally, I'll give you a new proverb, one I have found useful at times. Put not thy finger into thy neighbor's pie, lest it get stuck there permanently."

For the next few blocks, the silence between them was unbroken. Sally nodded to an occasional acquaintance, and Bobby, without lifting his eyes from the ground, seconded her salute with the mechanical raising of his hat which good breeding demands. Few conventions are more exasperatingly impersonal than the bow and smile of the average social being.

"But I love Beatrix," Sally said inconsequently, after an interval.

"I, too."

For the moment, both voices had lost their customary tone of light banter. Bobby broke the next pause.

"Couldn't you say something, Sally?"

"I wish I could; but it is no use. Beatrix hasn't the least respect for my opinion. She thinks I am only a child, and, moreover, once upon a time, I urged her to marry Mr. Lorimer. Of course, that was before any of this came out about him; but I hate to go into details with her, and, if I don't she will think it's nothing but a whim."

"What do you care what she thinks?"

Sally shifted her eyes from the apartment houses on Eighth Avenue to Bobby's face.

"Bobby, I am afraid of Beatrix," she confessed. "She is built on a larger frame than I am, and we both of us are quite aware of the fact."

"It may be a part of her capacious frame to risk her life in marrying Sidney Lorimer," Bobby grumbled; "but, for my part, I prefer smaller women."

Sally faced him suddenly.

"Bobby! You don't mean you think he will kill her sometime when he is drunk?"

"No such luck! In the intervals, he will adore her and treat her like a princess; but he won't spare her the anxiety and the shame of knowing he is liable to take too much at any reception to which they may send an acceptance. You haven't seen men as I have, Sally; you don't know how far they can make babbling fools of themselves, without being absolutely drunk. To a girl like Beatrix, the shame of it when it does occur, and the fear of the shame, when it doesn't, would be worse than sudden death. That gets over and done with; the other hangs on and grows worse and worse to an endless end."

"And you think there's no cure?"

Once more Bobby shrugged his shoulders.

"I wouldn't take any chances."

"You think Beatrix can't hold him?"

"She can for a time; but there's no knowing how long the time will last. Any medicine loses its effect, if it is repeated often enough."

"What about Mr. Thayer?"

"He has more power over Lorimer than anyone else; but he has his own professional life before him, and it won't be long before New York has a small share of his time. He isn't going to give up a grand success for the sake of playing keeper to Sidney Lorimer."

"I think he is fully capable of the sacrifice."

"Capable, yes. But it would be a sin to allow it; it would be spoiling a saint to patch up a sinner. Thayer's future is too broad to be limited by a futile creature like Lorimer. If he turns Quixotic, I'll poison him. At least, that will ensure his dying in the full tide of professional success."

"Ye-es," Sally answered thoughtfully; "but, do you know, Mr. Thayer is so perfectly organized that I have an idea he could swallow a certain amount of poison and come out of it unharmed, if his will were really bent upon accomplishing some definite end."

There was another interval. It was Sally's turn to break it.

"Bobby, does it occur to you that we are just exactly where we started? We both hate Mr. Lorimer; we hate the idea of his marrying Beatrix, and neither one of us dares interfere. Let's go and talk to Miss Gannion."

"What's the use?"

"To clear out our mental ganglia. At least, by the time we have been over it with her, we shall know what we think, and there's a certain satisfaction in that."

"I know just what I think about it now."

"What do you think?"

"Damn," Bobby replied concisely.

They found Miss Gannion alone before the fire. She threw down her book and welcomed them cordially.

"I had an indolent fit, to-day," she said, as she drew some chairs up before the hearth. "Once in a while, I prefer to dismiss my clerical adviser and settle my problems to suit myself. To be sure, I am quite likely to settle them wrongly; but that renews my confidence in churchly methods, so some good is gained, after all."

Bobby deliberately placed himself in the chair which long experience of Miss Gannion's house had taught him best fitted the angles of his anatomy.

"We came to have you settle a problem for us," he said; "so we are glad your hand is in."

"And the problem," Sally added; "is Beatrix."

"What about Beatrix?" Miss Gannion asked.

"She is going to marry Sidney Lorimer, and she mustn't. Please tell us how we are going to prevent it."

Miss Gannion sat still for a moment, with her clear eyes fixed on the glowing embers.

"Are you sure that it would be best to prevent it?" she asked then.

Bobby started to his feet, faced about, and stood looking down at the little figure of his hostess.

"Miss Gannion, Beatrix and I have been chums ever since we could go alone. In fact, we learned to go alone by hanging on to each other's hands. I love her as a fellow without any sisters is bound to love a girl cousin; and I'll be blest if I can keep quiet and see her throw herself away."

"Have you spoken to her about it?"

"I don't dare," Bobby returned bluntly. "I know I should end by losing my temper and saying things about Lorimer. I wouldn't hurt Beatrix for the world, and I believe she honestly thinks she is doing the Lord's own work in not throwing Lorimer over."

"Perhaps she may be," Miss Gannion said gently.

"Miss Gannion! Well, if she is, I shall have to revise my notions of the Lord," Bobby responded hotly.

Miss Gannion's smile never wavered. She knew Bobby Dane too well to resent his occasional outbursts.

"Bobby, my dear boy," she said, with the maternal accent she assumed at times; "this isn't too easy a problem for any of us; but the hardest part of its solution is coming on Beatrix. It's not an easy place to put a woman with a conscience. The old-fashioned idea was to marry a man to reform him; the new-fashioned practice is to wash your hands of him altogether, as soon as he makes a single slip. The middle course is the most difficult one to take and the most thankless. Any good woman is sure to have a strong hold on the man who loves her; and, in times of real danger, she is afraid to let go that hold."

Bobby shook his head.

"That's Beatrix all over, Miss Gannion. But it will take a mighty strong grip to haul Lorimer across to firm ground."

"I realize that."

"But the question is, does Beatrix realize it, too," Sally said abruptly.

"Better than we can. I think she has measured both the danger and her own strength."

Bobby took a turn or two up and down the room. Then he came back to the hearthrug.

"She can't do it," he said conclusively. "The odds are all against her. Lorimer can't pull her down, of course; but he can tug and tug till he has used up all her strength and she has to let him go. And then what? Miss Gannion, do you honestly think it worth the while?"

"No; I do not," she said reluctantly.

"Then why the deuce do you argue for it?" he asked, with a recurrence of his former temper. "I beg your pardon, Miss Gannion; but this maddens me, and I came here to have you help me find a way out. Instead, you are in favor of Beatrix's signing her own death warrant."

"No," she said slowly. "Down in my heart of hearts, I think it is all a mistake, a terrible mistake; and I have tried in vain to find a way to prevent it. Then, each time I think it over, I am afraid to prevent it, because it seems to me that Beatrix's mistake is just a little bit nobler than the safe course which we ourselves would take."

"Have you heard Mr. Thayer say what he thinks about it?" Sally asked.

"Not lately."

Sally's eyes were under less subjection than her tongue, and Miss Gannion answered the question they so plainly asked.

"Long ago, before the night of the concert, even, Mr. Thayer spoke of the matter to me. Since then he has never mentioned it."

"I wish you would ask him what he thinks now," Sally said bluntly. "He knows Mr. Lorimer better than any of us do, and he should be able to judge what we ought to do about it."

"The honest fact is," Bobby broke in thoughtfully; "we can't one of us do a solitary thing about it, but get together and grumble. Beatrix hasn't a clinging, confiding nature; she makes up her own mind and she doesn't change it easily. If she has decided to marry Lorimer, we can kneel in a ring at her feet and shed tears by the pint, and all the good it will do us will be the chance of making her die of pneumonia caused by the surrounding dampness. But it's a beastly shame! I'd rather she married Arlt and done with it. If you've got to form a character, it's better to start in while the character is young."

Miss Gannion caught at the opportunity for a digression.

"Mr. Arlt is coming to lunch," she observed.

"To-day? I didn't know he was back in town."

"He came last night."

"Was Mr. Thayer with him?"

"No; Mr. Thayer sings in Boston, last night and to-night. He sent me a note, saying I might expect him to dinner on Tuesday."

"I wonder what success Mr. Arlt has had."

"Mr. Thayer sent me some criticisms. They were very enthusiastic, as far as they went; but that was only a few lines."

"And the rest of the criticism probably concerned itself with Thayer, and was discreetly cut away," Bobby said, as he dropped back into his chair. "Miss Gannion, Arlt is on the steps, and you have not invited us to stay to lunch, so we must take a reluctant departure. Before I go, though, I'd like to ask one favor. When Thayer comes, Tuesday night, are you willing to talk the whole matter over with him and see what he thinks about it now? There would be a certain consolation to me in knowing that he disapproved the affair, and he may possibly suggest some way of breaking it off."

"Possibly," Miss Gannion assented; "unless it is already too late."

The words were still ringing in the air, when Arlt came into the room. They were still ringing in Bobby's ears, ten minutes later, when he and Sally took their leave.

"My mental ganglia are cleared," Bobby said disconsolately, as they went down the steps. "I now see that there is precisely one thing for us to do, and only one."

"What is that?"

"To grin and bear it."

CHAPTER ELEVEN

Beatrix's principles extended even to the point of observing her day at home. Society was bidden, the next afternoon, to a tea at Mrs. Stanley's, and Beatrix was absolutely certain that none of her friends would cross the intervening forty blocks in order to look in upon her, going or coming. In her secret heart, she longed to follow society; instead, she was sitting in solitude, when Thayer was announced.

She rose to greet him with a cordial friendliness, for the past six months had made a great change in their outward relations. They had liked each other from the day of Mrs. Stanley's recital, and the liking had increased with each subsequent meeting. During the next few weeks, they had met often. Lorimer insisted upon going to every recital at which Thayer was to sing, and under his guidance Beatrix had gained a fair idea of what went on behind the scenes. Thayer, meanwhile, had swiftly assumed his own place in society, and discerning hostesses generally found it well to put him near to Beatrix at dinner. Owing to his many evening engagements, Thayer usually ate but sparingly, so it was all the more necessary that he should be placed within range of someone with whom he cared to talk. He rarely lent himself to the usual run of social badinage; but retired into his shell whenever it became the dominant note of the conversation. A man of his bulk and prominence and potential boredom was an object of hospitable consideration. He could always talk to Beatrix, for she never chattered. Therefore he was generally to be found somewhere within the conversational radius of Beatrix Dane.

The tea table of Beatrix, moreover, had become one of the focal points of his New York life. He liked the cheery, informal atmosphere of the house whose old-fashioned austerity was tempered with a dash of modern frivolity; he liked the people he met there, people too assured of their own social position to be touchy upon slight points of social precedence. Most of all, he liked Beatrix Dane, herself. In the gay, chattering multitude among whom she moved, her own steadfast quietness stood out in bold relief, and it answered to certain traits of his own Puritanism. It was not that she was dull, or overfreighted with conscience. She frisked with the others of her kind; but her friskiness was intermittent and never frivolous. To Beatrix Dane, pleasure was an interlude, never the sole end and aim of life. And, on her own side, Beatrix felt a thorough admiration for the clean-minded, clean-bodied singer, a thorough reliance upon his judgment and upon his loyalty to anyone to whom he vouchsafed his friendship.

This had been the relation between them, on the evening of the concert for the Fresh Air Fund, a relation whose cordial matter-of-factness was in no way disturbed by the potent spell of Thayer's voice. Beatrix had spent much of her life in the open air; she was too healthy to be given to self-analysis. She admitted to herself the wonderful power of Thayer's voice, the passionate appeal of certain of his songs; but she made a curiously sharp distinction between the man and the voice. The one might be a strong guiding force in the current of her life; the other was a rising tide that swept her from her moorings and left her drifting to and fro over stormy seas. On the night of the Fresh Air Fund concert, for the first time in her experience, these two personalities had become inextricably intermingled. As she had said, she had never before realized the possibilities of either Thayer or his voice.

Everything had conspired to produce the impression. All day long, she had been haunted by a nervous, nameless dread. The vague hints and signs of the past months had suddenly gathered to a nucleus of anxiety and alarm, and, in spite of her rigid self-control, she had been terrified into giving the one outcry, partly to satisfy her feminine need for sympathy, partly with the hope of putting Lorimer upon his guard. The sympathy had come, prompt and loving; the warning had been utterly ignored.

Music ought to be taken with fasting and prayer. Quiet nerves and a full stomach are deaf to its deepest meaning. To most of the audience, *Honor and Arms* stood as a superb piece of vocal gymnastics; to Beatrix, Thayer was like a live wire, pulsing with a virile scorn of any but uneven contests, defiant only of those mightier than himself. To her mind, he was ready to court heavy odds, bound to conquer them, one and all; and her own pulses beat faster in time to the half-barbarous outburst which ends the great aria. The Gade concerto, instead of soothing her, had only exasperated her. She longed to get behind the violinist and the orchestra and even the composer himself, and goad them into some tenseness of emotion. But the Slavonic Dance had set her heart bounding once more, until her very finger tips tingled with the blood racing through them, and the clashing cymbals had seemed scarcely louder than the ringing of her own ears. The rest had been only the natural sequel; *Danny* and Arlt's failure had led inevitably up to the finale when Thayer's eyes, burning with that new, strange light, had held her own eyes captive while he had sounded the tragic note which dominates all human love.

And the finale had not been final, after all. She had had a vague presentiment that the cross might be at the end; she had been totally unprepared to find it pressed to her lips, that selfsame night.

With a swift excuse, Thayer had hurried her back into the music-room; but he had not been able to prevent that one instant when Beatrix had found herself face to face with a Lorimer she had never known till then. Though her eyes had betrayed her horror of the scene, she had kept her voice steady as she asked Thayer to call her carriage and to say her farewells to her hostess.

Thayer went with her to her own door. Neither of them spoke until they stood on the steps; then Thayer cleared his throat, but even then his voice was husky.

"It may not be as bad as you think, Miss Dane," he said slowly.

As if with a physical effort, she raised her eyes to his.

"Perhaps not," she assented; "but I can think of nothing worse."

It took Thayer two weeks to gather together his courage to see her again. He too had been shaken by the events of the evening. His Slav blood, kindled by the Dvorák dance, fired by his anger for Arlt, had blazed up into a fury of scorn and hatred against the man who would so allow his own weakness to stab another's strength. Lorimer, in Bobby Dane's cab and under the lash of Bobby's energetic tongue, was out of Thayer's way; but, as Thayer stood looking down at the face, whiter than the fluffy white fur of her cloak, he had felt a momentary longing to take Beatrix into his arms and, holding her there, to protect her from Lorimer and from the danger that was threatening her whole happiness. The moment passed and with it the longing; but, unknown to himself, it had done its work. It had broken out the beginning of a new channel; it had prepared the way for a new trend of thought.

Bobby Dane told him what had actually passed between himself and Lorimer on the way home, what had probably occurred, the next day, between Lorimer and Beatrix. Thayer waited before calling until he hoped the memory of what had passed was so remote that neither he nor Beatrix would think of it again. Nevertheless, though Beatrix was surrounded by callers and upon her guard, the eyes of both drooped before the sudden consciousness of having faced a crisis side by side.

According to their annual custom, the Danes went to their cottage at Monomoy, the first of July, and Lorimer took up his quarters at the hotel, less than a mile away. Two weeks later, Thayer and Arlt joined him there. Lorimer had been urgent for Thayer's coming, and Thayer, upon thinking the matter over, could see no valid reason for refusal. Miss Gannion was on the way to Alaska, that summer, and, next to her, the Danes were the closest friends he had made during his first season in New York. It was only natural that he should arrange his plans in order to be near them. Moreover, the idle life on the island sounded attractive, and he was fully aware of the fact that his constant companionship would be a strong hold upon Lorimer. All in all, he decided to go.

He took Arlt with him, on the plea of requiring an accompanist for the new songs he was studying. The boy needed the change. The stress of New York life was wearing upon him; the consciousness of comparative failure had disheartened him. He needed the tonic of sea air and of idleness and of contact with inartistic, care-free humanity. Furthermore, Thayer felt that he himself might need the tonic of the simple-hearted affection of the young German. The world about him was too complex. There were days when the most conventional of incidents seemed weighted with a hidden meaning, burdened with a consciousness of their own future import.

The summer days passed swiftly and with a certain monotony. During the mornings while Thayer was practising, Lorimer and Beatrix idled away the hours together. Later in the day, Thayer always appeared at Monomoy, sometimes with Lorimer, sometimes alone. Occasionally Beatrix forsook them both, and went off for long walks with Arlt or floated lazily about the harbor with him, leaving her mother to entertain the young men with garrulous recollections of her own childhood.

One subject was forever sealed between Beatrix and Thayer, to one evening's events they neither of them ever alluded. Now and then, at some careless turn of the conversation, one or the other of them would stealthily raise his eyes to find the other furtively watching him; and their eyes would drop apart again swiftly. It was obvious to Thayer that Beatrix was carrying a heavy care, that summer. If Lorimer were tardy in appearing, she was absent and restless; if he came upon her suddenly, she started; if he talked or laughed more than usual, she invented an excuse to take him away from the group, apart from the general conversation. Occasionally, it was evident to Thayer that she was trying to take him, himself, off his guard, seeking to make him betray himself, in case he was sharing in her watchfulness. Upon such occasions, Thayer's mental armor became as impenetrable as a corselet of steel. If he were keeping guard over Lorimer, amusing him and circumventing him in a thousand different ways, it was not only for Lorimer's sake, but for that of Beatrix as well, and it was imperative that Beatrix should never know. The day had passed forever when he could look into Miss Gannion's clear eyes and declare with perfect truthfulness that Beatrix was nothing in the world to him. He admitted this to himself; he also admitted that there are an infinite number of gradations between the opposite poles, nothing and something. There was no especial need of deciding which one of them marked his present status.

This Monday afternoon was the first time he had seen Beatrix since early September. He had left the others at Monomoy and, in company with Arlt, had gone back to the city to put himself in training for some autumn festivals at which he had been engaged to sing. By the time Beatrix was back in town once more, he had started upon what was destined to be a triumphal progress through New England. To some men, the mere professional success would have been enough in itself; but Thayer was of too large calibre to find a steady diet of applause and adjectives, both in the superlative degree of comparison, either a satisfactory or a stimulating meal. Often and often, as he bowed across the footlights preparatory to shouldering and lugging off his ponderous wreath of laurels, he would have given all the evening's triumph for the sake of one quiet hour upon the Monomoy beach.

The evening before had been the climax of his empty successes. It had been Boston's first oratorio of the season, and the wreath had been an unusually ponderous one. It had met him promptly at the end of his first number, and it had impressed him as a curious bit of irony, following as it did upon the closing phrases of *Spe modo Vivitur*. Were his crowns to be only the thornless, characterless ones that went with his profession? He bowed low, nevertheless, before the storm of applause, set up his trophy against the steadiest of the music racks of the second violins, and lost himself so completely in wondering how Lorimer was holding out without him that he went through his part in the quartette, three numbers later, in perfect unconsciousness of the hostile glances which the soprano had been casting at him during the *Est tibi Laurea*. Her flowers had been carnations, and only two dozen of them, at that.

The next afternoon, Thayer found himself in the familiar room, with Beatrix's hand in his own.

"Only ten weeks, measured by time," he answered her greeting; "but it seems half a decade since we were killing time on the beach at Monomoy."

"Killing crabs, you would better say," she returned, with a smile. "I think you and Sidney must have exterminated the race for all time."

"Can you destroy the future for a race that habitually goes backwards?" he questioned, with a boyish gayety which she had never seen in him before. "How is Lorimer?"

No one else but Thayer would have noted the slight hesitation that punctuated her reply.

"He is--well."

Thayer's momentary gayety left him, and he glanced at her sharply.

"And you?" he asked.

"I am always in rude health, just now the better for having you invade my loneliness. Do you still take only one lump?" Her tone was perfectly noncommittal.

"Only one. How does it happen that I have the good luck to find you alone?"

"Everybody is at Mrs. Stanley's. She has captured a new lion, and has bidden the world to come and inspect her prey."

Thayer laughed.

"What is he, this time?"

"Not he at all; it is a full-fledged Japanese princess whose husband does lectures on some sort of theosophy before all the universities. Your lustre is totally eclipsed by this new comet." There was a short silence; then Beatrix added inconsequently, "We all of us have been so delighted at your success, Mr. Thayer."

He did not take the trouble to discount the fact; but merely asked,--

"How did you know about it?"

"We have followed you in the papers. Bobby had some, and I think Sidney must have bought tons of them. He even talked of subscribing to a clipping bureau. He has read them aloud to us, every night; and we all have tried to act as if it were nothing so very unusual to have one of our friends winning laurels by the wholesale."

"They were very concrete laurels, too, Miss Dane," he returned indifferently, though his face had lighted at her eager accent. "Some of the wreaths must have been four feet across, and I invariably tripped over the ribbons, when I carried them off the stage. I did wish they would furnish a dray; garlands are horribly in the way in a carriage."

"And then what became of them?"

Thayer shrugged his shoulders.

"Ask the chambermaids along the route. I don't mean to be unappreciative; but not even the most trusting of publics could expect me to bear my trophies away in my arms, next morning. I came to wish I could ship them back to the florist, to be presented to some other baritone, the next night."

"But you enjoyed the trip?"

"After a fashion. I enjoyed the summer more, though."

"There is a certain satisfaction in dropping off the social harness now and then, and we were comparatively primitive at Monomoy," she assented. "The whole summer would have been worth while, just for the sake of seeing Mr. Arlt enjoy it. Has he come back yet?"

"Yes, two days ago. The trip has meant a good deal to him, and already he is engaged for two festivals in the spring. I am hoping that a taste of success will give him more self-reliance. He needs it, if ever he is to impose himself upon the dear public. Even the critics are prone to take a man at his own valuation, and one of the best American musicians is working in a corner, to-day, because he finds it a good deal more interesting to work towards future successes than to exploit his past ones in the eyes of the world."

Beatrix smiled, half in assent, half in amusement at his sudden energy.

"Mr. Arlt will succeed in time; he is only a boy yet. But, with genius and energy and his real love for his art, there can be no doubt of his future."

"That is as fate may decree," Thayer answered.

"Or Providence," she corrected him.

He shook his head.

"Miss Dane, the more I know of life, I am learning to write fate in capitals, and to spell Providence with a little *p*. Things are pretty well cut out for us."

She glanced at him with sudden intentness.

"Then I hope the scissors are sharp, and that Moira carries a steady hand. We have to put up with our own indecisions; those of other people are maddening."

"Doesn't that depend upon what the decision finally proves to be?" he asked.

Her eyes had gone back to the fire, and her face was very grave.

"No; I would rather know where I am going. Anything is better than drifting; it is a comfort to look steadily forward to the best or to the worst." Suddenly she roused herself. "Mr. Thayer, do you realize that it is two months since I have heard you sing?"

He roused himself quite as suddenly. In the slight pause which had broken her speech, he had been making a swift, but futile effort to chart the future. He knew that Lorimer was drifting carelessly, thoughtlessly; he also knew that Beatrix was allowing herself to drift idly in his wake. And how about himself? And would they all make the same port in the end? If not, where would the diverging currents be waiting for them?

His brain was working intently; but his voice was quite conventional, as he rose.

"I hoped you would ask me. After a month or two of singing to strangers, I begin to feel the need of something a little more personal. Will you have the new songs, or the old?"

"The old, of course," she answered unhesitatingly.

He improvised for a moment; then he began to sing,--

"*The hours I spent with thee, dear heart, Are as a string of pearls to me. I count them over one by--*"

Abruptly he stopped singing and struck a dozen resonant major chords.

"What a disgustingly sentimental thing that is!" he said sharply. "After our summer at Monomoy in the sea air, we need an atmosphere of ozone, not of laughing gas."

And he played the prelude of *Die Beiden Grenadieren*.

CHAPTER TWELVE

Arlt dropped in at Thayer's rooms, the next afternoon, and sat looking on while his friend put himself into his evening clothes, preparatory to dining with Miss Gannion.

"I walked up here with Mr. Dane," he observed, after a thoughtful interval. "What an American he is!"

"American?"

"Yes. No other country but yours can produce such people. France tries it, and fails. A Frenchman takes his frivolity in earnest. Mr. Dane is like that little *Scherzo* by Faulkes, the one that frisks on and on, and all of a sudden comes to an end with a loud *Ha ha* over its own absurdity. Mr. Dane delights in his own talk, just as you delight in your singing."

"He is not self-conscious," Thayer objected quickly.

"Neither are you. Each of you has a gift, and you each delight in using it. That is not saying that you either of you regard it as the only gift in the world. Instead, having it, you make the most of it, to let it grow and to put it in the way of giving pleasure to other people."

Thayer smiled, in spite of himself.

"To paraphrase you, Arlt, what a German you are! Nobody else would attempt to philosophize concerning Bobby Dane."

"Why not? He is worth it, for he has other gifts than his wit."

"Did he say anything about Lorimer?" Thayer asked abruptly.

"He spoke of him once or twice."

"Anything especial?"

"N-o."

There had been a slight hesitation. The next instant, Arlt felt Thayer's keen eyes upon him.

"Is anything wrong with Lorimer?"

"What should there be?"

"Nothing should be. I asked if anything is."

"Mr. Dane would hardly discuss his friends with me." Arlt's tone was noncommittal.

"Now, see here, Arlt, don't get obstinate. We both know Lorimer's failing. Have you heard anything new about him?"

Arlt stared hard at the carpet.

"Mr. Lorimer was very good to the mother and Katarina," he said, in his slow, deliberate English.

"That may be. Mr. Lorimer has been good to a great many people, and we aren't going to forget it. That doesn't keep us from knowing his weakness."

"No," Arlt said simply; "but it might keep us from discussing it."

Thayer's lips shut closely for an instant. He felt a rebuke which Arlt would never have dared to intend.

"It might; but it does not. We both know it, and there is no harm in our talking it over. Lorimer is weak and foolish; he isn't nearly so bad as many men we know. The taint is in his blood, and he is too easy-going to fight it out."

"But he did fight, last summer," Arlt urged.

Thayer's thoughts flew backwards to one night, in Lorimer's room at the hotel. It seemed to him he could still see Lorimer's flushed face, still hear against the background of noises that marred the stillness of the August moonlight outside the window, the high-pitched, insistent voice of the man who sat on the edge of the bed, arguing about the necessity of unlacing his shoes before taking them off. The next morning, Beatrix had received a note from Thayer, apologizing for carrying Lorimer off for a day's fishing. Cotton Mather himself might well have envied the grim fervor of the sermon preached by his namesake, that sunshiny summer day. The old-time hell gave place to a more modern theory of retribution; but the terrors were painted with a black-tipped brush, and Lorimer had shuddered, as he listened. For the once, Thayer had made no effort to avoid rousing his antagonism. Lorimer had been more angry than ever before in his life; then the inevitable reaction had come, and it had been a penitent, hopeful sinner who had walked up the pier at Thayer's side, late in the afternoon. But Arlt, who had been playing Chopin at Monomoy, all the previous evening, was quite at a loss to understand how a single day's fishing could so completely exhaust a strong man like Thayer.

Arlt changed his phrase to the direct question.

"Don't you think he fought with the best that was in him?"

And Thayer assented with perfect truthfulness,--

"I do."

"Then we ought to ask for nothing more."

"If he stood alone. Unfortunately he doesn't."

Arlt raised his brows.

"But the risk is hers."

Thayer untied his necktie with a long, deliberate pull, and made a second attempt to arrange it to his liking. At length he turned from the mirror and faced Arlt.

"Would you be willing to allow Katarina to take such a risk?"

"No," Arlt answered honestly, after an interval.

Neither man spoke for some time. Arlt was unwilling to continue the subject, and Thayer knew from experience the uselessness of trying to force him to talk when he was minded to keep silence. It was Arlt, however, who finally broke the silence, and his subject was one utterly remote from Lorimer.

"I have heard from the mother, to-day," he said suddenly.

"Good news, I hope." Thayer's tone was as hearty as if he had felt no passing annoyance at the boy's stubborn reticence.

"The best that can be for them. An old cousin has died, and they are his heirs."

"Good! Is it much?"

"Enough so they can live in comfort, whatever happens to me."

"And enough so that you can live in comfort, without anxiety for them," Thayer supplemented kindly.

"Without anxiety; I can do without the comfort," Arlt replied. "I have worried sometimes."

Crossing the room, Thayer laid his hand on the boy's shoulder.

"And you have borne the worry very pluckily, too, Arlt. It has been hard for you, this first year in America, with the double care for them and for yourself. I hope things are going to be easier now."

"It will be a help in my work," he assented. Then he added, with a sudden effort which showed how dear the subject was to his heart, "I think I shall now have a few more lessons in counterpoint."

"More?" Thayer said interrogatively.

"Yes; I had already studied for two years."

"And you want to compose?"

"When I know enough. Not till then."

"It takes something besides the knowing, to make a composer, Arlt," Thayer said warningly.

"I know. But I think I have something to say, when I am ready," the boy answered, with simple directness.

"But, if you wanted to study counterpoint, why didn't you say so? You knew I would lend you the money."

"Yes, you would give me everything; but I could never accept this."

"Why not?"

Arlt looked up, and even Thayer, well as he knew him, was surprised at the sudden concentration of character in the boy's face.

"One will be helped in the small things, never in accomplishing the real purpose of his life. Each one of us must work that out for himself. Then, if he succeeds or fails, at least the result is of his own making."

Dismissing four or five importunate cab drivers with a brief shake of his head, Thayer went striding away up the Avenue towards Miss Gannion's house. As he went, he was half-consciously applying Arlt's words to the question of his own future. It was true enough that he must work out his own real purpose for himself; and, in one sense the unsuccessful boy was happier by far than the successful man. Arlt's purpose was single. Thayer's was two-fold, and as yet he could not determine which of them would prove to be the dominant impulse of his life.

"Really, it does seem very good to drop back into the old ways," Miss Gannion said contentedly, two hours later.

The loitering, lingering dinner was over; the servants had been instructed to admit no other guests, and Miss Gannion was snuggled back in her deep chair, gazing up at Thayer who stood on the rug with his hands idly locked behind his back. In this room which showed so plainly its feminine occupancy, he seemed uncommonly virile, and Miss Gannion, watching him, felt a momentary exultation in his virility. Most of the men whom she knew, put on a feminine languor as an adjunct to their evening clothes. Thayer looked down upon her with manifest approval. After months of separation, it was good to find himself in the presence of this woman to whom he was allowed to speak freely his real opinion. Miss Gannion by no means always agreed with him; but she usually understood his point of view and was willing to admit its weight. Moreover, she was able to discuss without losing her temper, and she belonged to that species of good listener who understands that an occasional word of comprehension is worth more than hours of mere silent attention.

"It is refreshing to get back to a place where my personality counts for something," Thayer assured her. "The past two months have left me feeling as if I had not a friend in the world, nothing but audiences."

"What an ingrate you are! Most of us would be willing to have that kind of impersonality."

"Would you?"

"No," she said candidly. "I'm not large enough for that."

"It wouldn't have occurred to me that it was any indication of largeness."

"To be able to resign your own individuality, for the sake of the pleasure you can give other people? That seems to me rather large."

"It depends. I think I would rather concentrate my efforts, person on person, instead of spreading myself out like a vast impersonal plaster."

She laughed a little, though her eyes were very grave.

"You might apply your theory here and now. Go and sing to me, not a new song, but one of the old favorites."

Obediently he crossed the room to the piano where he sat for an hour, now singing, now stopping to comment on a song or to relate some of his experiences of the past two months. Later that night, when Miss Gannion was thinking over the talk of the evening, it suddenly occurred to her that he had made no reference at all to the summer. At length he rose to return to the fire.

"No," she objected. "There is one song still lacking. You've not sung *The Rosary* yet."

His stride across the room never hesitated, although duller ears than his own could not have mistaken the wish in her voice.

"I have worn out *The Rosary*," he said briefly. "I shall have to let it rest for a while."

"I am sorry. I loved it."

He laughed mirthlessly.

"It is the weakest kind of sentimentality, Miss Gannion. The song itself amounts to very little; it is merely a question of the key."

"I am sorry," she repeated, still a little sadly. "I have cared a good deal for the song."

Thayer made no answer, and she sat looking up at him with a steady wishfulness which made him uneasy. Her next words, though chosen by chance, increased his uneasiness.

"Have you seen Miss Dane, since you came back?"

"I was there, yesterday."

"How did she seem to you?"

His steady eyes met hers without wavering.

"I don't quite understand what you mean by the question."

Miss Gannion varied the form of her words.

"Did you think she looked well?"

"Very."

"And yet, I don't think Beatrix is happy," Miss Gannion said, half to herself.

"Why not?"

"How can she be? Beatrix is not dense. She thinks things, and she must know the uncertainty of the future."

"But I thought it was quite certain." There was a level monotony in Thayer's accent.

"You think Mr. Lorimer has really reformed and is out of danger?" Miss Gannion asked quickly.

"I wish he had," Thayer answered half involuntarily.

"Then there is still trouble?"

But already Thayer was once more upon his guard.

"I have heard of nothing since I came home."

"Have you seen Mr. Lorimer?"

"No."

There was a curt brevity in his manner which was new to Miss Gannion. In spite of herself, it set her to wondering whether prosperity had been good for her friend, whether the consciousness of his own importance were making him indifferent to the interests of others. Perhaps, after all, it was true that he was becoming impersonal. He might be growing larger; he was certainly growing more remote from her life. Miss Gannion cared for Thayer. Now, while she watched him, her eyes were lighted with an almost fierce affection, even though her disappointment made her voice take on a hard, metallic ring, as she asked,--

"Are you turning your back upon the problem of your old friend, Mr. Thayer?"

"No," he answered; "but I thought we had solved it, in this very room."

She raised her brows interrogatively.

"'To say our prayers, and wait,'" he quoted.

Her momentary distrust of him weakened, and her face lighted, as she heard him quoting her own words, spoken so long ago.

"Yes; but I--we all--think it is time--think it may be a mistake."

He lifted his eyes from the fire, looked at her steadily for a minute, and then stared into the fire again. She grew restless with the stillness.

"And we thought perhaps you could say something."

"To--?" he asked, without raising his eyes.

"To Mr. Lorimer."

"What could I say?"

"Something to break it off."

In spite of himself, he laughed outright.

"Would you advise threats or bribery, Miss Gannion? I really can't imagine any argument that would lead Lorimer to give up Miss Dane of his own accord."

"Couldn't you put it to him strongly that he has no moral right to hold her to her promise?"

"I could; but he would probably put it to me just as strongly that I have no moral right to interfere in his concerns."

Miss Gannion sat up straight, bracing her elbows against the sides of her chair.

"Mr. Thayer, have you any idea that Mr. Lorimer will ever give up drinking, drinking more than is good for him?"

"I have not."

"Have you any idea that Beatrix, if she marries him, can escape years of anxiety and wretchedness?"

"I have not," he answered again.

"Oh, how cold you are!" she cried, in passionate revolt against his even tone. "Don't you care anything at all for Beatrix?"

If he flinched at her question, he rallied again too quickly for her to discover it. Then he looked her squarely in the eye.

"I would do anything in my power to protect Miss Dane; but this is a case where I have no right to speak to her. I have spoken to Lorimer again and again, urging him to control himself for her sake. Beyond that, I have no right to go."

"But you said once that you thought she ought to be told."

"That was months ago. She found out, without being told."

"Not all."

"Enough."

"But, if she knew all about it, all that you know, Beatrix Dane would never marry Sidney Lorimer."

"Very likely not."

"Then you ought to tell her. What right have you to suppress facts that would change her whole point of view? You have it in your power to save Beatrix Dane. Once you were willing to do it." She had risen and stood on the rug, facing him. Stung by his coldness and by her disappointment in him, she allowed a sudden note of hostility to creep into her voice, and it cut Thayer like the edge of a steel knife.

"I am sorry," he said, after a pause; "but it is too late for that now, Miss Gannion."

His words were more true than he realized. When, after a half-hour of uncomfortable, disjointed talk, he said good-night and went away, he found Lorimer waiting for him in his own rooms. Thayer's greeting was curt, for he was still smarting from the memory of his talk with Miss Gannion. He had been impenetrable to her questions, but not to her sharpness, and he was hurt by the disapproval she had shown. It was the first time he had heard the curious icy tone in her voice; it had struck a jarring note in their friendship. For the time being, Miss Gannion had distrusted him; but at least she had gained no idea of the cause of his changed attitude. For so much, he was thankful. He had saved his own respect at the risk of forfeiting that of Miss Gannion.

Lorimer met him excitedly; but Thayer's experienced eye saw that the excitement had no alcoholic basis.

"Congratulations, old fellow! Everything is settled at last, and we are to be married, early in January. I came straight to you, for I knew you would be delighted. Of course, I shall count on you as best man."

It would never have occurred to Thayer that there was need to brace himself against any possible shock. For a minute, the droplight on the table seemed to be dancing a Russian *trépac*. Then, just as it was ready to fall, he heard his own voice saying, with exactly the proper degree of cordiality,--

"I do congratulate you, Lorimer, and I am delighted that it is settled."

Later on, he knew that he had spoken the truth.

"And you will be best man?" Lorimer questioned eagerly.

"Yes. Who else has better claim?" The conventional note was still there; Thayer felt its aloofness far more than Lorimer, absorbed in his own joy, was able to do. The silence was short; then Thayer mastered himself again. "Lorimer," he said quietly; "I certainly do congratulate you, for you have been able to gain one of the noblest women in the world. Your happiness ought to be great; but you have taken a fearful responsibility along with it. At your best you can be worthy of her; but, if you fall one inch below your best level, you will deserve to be flayed alive. You have gone into this with your eyes open. You know that you can make Beatrix Dane's life a heaven or a hell. You and I both know the danger; we know that she is running a terrible risk in marrying you, and that you yourself are the only person who can save her from shame and sorrow. For God's sake, Lorimer, do all you can to make yourself live up to the best that is in you."

CHAPTER THIRTEEN

Late March found Thayer just completing a long circle. He had gone to Chicago by way of Washington; he was coming back by way of Canada and New England. Oratorio societies were rampant, that Lent, and he had been the popular baritone of the season, completely ousting from public favor the bass who had monopolized the applause for six or seven years previous. He had fainted under Elijah's juniper tree times without number, until he had learned to watch with cynical interest for the phrase which never failed to draw forth the tears. He had even taken part in one grand operatic rendition of the work, when the audience had been half strangled by the too realistic fumes from the altar, and the chorus, huddled at the back of the stage, had sung the *Rain Chorus* off the key, to the accompaniment of the torrent which poured down in a thin sheet just back of the curtain, raining neither on the just nor on the unjust, but falling accurately into the groove for the footlights between them. He had sung *The Messiah* and *Arminius* until they were a weariness to his flesh, and *Hiawatha's* call to *Gitche Manito, the Mighty* had become second nature to his tongue. He had moments of acute longing to astound his audience with a German student song, and, upon his off nights, he fell into the vaudeville habit. Not even his Puritanism could enjoy an unlimited diet of oratorio.

At first there had been some question of his giving a number of recitals at different points on his journey; but he had renounced the idea. Arlt was grinding away at counterpoint under the best master to be found in New York, and Arlt was the only accompanist with whom Thayer cared to sing. The boy had no notion that Thayer needed him; neither did he have any idea of the discrepancy between his own payments and the actual fees of the great musician with whom Thayer had advised him to study. Week by week, he brought his few dollars, without once suspecting that Thayer's monthly checks were really paying for the lessons.

Arlt had fallen to work with the eagerness born of long and enforced abstinence. Certain musical themes had been haunting him for the past two years; yet he had known that he lacked the training which should enable him to develop them properly, and, with rare self-denial, rather than spoil them he had turned his back upon them and tried to forget them. Now, however, his work was beginning to tell upon him, and his teacher was more and more encouraging, while the old themes came back to him, grown and enriched by their season of lying fallow. Spurred on by the consciousness of all this, Arlt was hard at work upon an overture with which he hoped to greet Thayer on his return to the city. Day by day, the overture was growing. It was boyish; yet it was dignified and original.

On the last morning of his trip, Thayer came down the steps of his hotel, halted to stare about him at the streets of the leisurely little city, and then sauntered away towards the hall where the rehearsal was to take place. It was still early; nevertheless, as he came within sight of the building, he found the street filled with the members of the orchestra who, thriftily refusing cabs, had marched up from the station in a solid phalanx, laden with all manner of strange-looking bags and cases. Thayer nodded to them with a certain eagerness. After two months of wandering, it was good to find himself once more within the New York radius. He had sung with these men often; they knew every trick of his voice, and he could count upon them not to break into a galloping rhythm in the midst of a minor *andante*. His face lighted, and his tongue fell into his beloved German idioms, as he went up the stairs with a bass viol and a bassoon on either hand.

The director of the chorus was also a New York man, and Thayer shook hands with him cordially, wondering, meanwhile, how it chanced that one short year had made him feel that New York was home to him. The director knew Arlt's teacher, too. He had heard of the young German's promise, and it was with some regret that Thayer heard him break off from these congenial themes, for the sake of introducing him to the officers of the society who were unduly agitated by the consciousness that they had captured both Thayer and the latest English tenor who had landed only the week before and was to make his American début, that evening.

Meanwhile, the hall was filling fast. The chorus, chattering with the nervous vivacity which always heralds a concert, were crowding into the fraction of space allotted to them; and, in the open floor beyond, the musicians of the orchestra were gathered into little groups, unpacking their instruments, unfolding their racks and eying the chorus with metropolitan disdain. Here and there a violinist, his violin at his shoulder, sauntered up and down the floor, alternately drawing his bow across the strings and lowering it again, while he tightened them. Then, in answer to the call from the oboe, the whole place grew filled with their din, discordant at first, but slowly coming into more and more perfect harmony, uniting upon the single note, breaking again into countless changing tones, only to yield once more to the single *A*, caught, dropped during an instant's pause, then caught again and held in long-drawn, jubilant sonority.

On the heels of the other soloists, Thayer picked his way up the narrow aisle at the right of the tenors, and took his seat upon the little stage. As he did so, he discovered a diminutive gallery directly over the main entrance to the hall. Side by side in the gallery sat two men, the president of the chorus and Bobby Dane.

Bobby was beaming down at him placidly, and Thayer's face lighted at the unexpected sight of his friend. Bobby nodded occasionally, to mark his approval of the music; then, at the end of Thayer's first solo, he laid his score on the gallery rail and led off a volley of applause which, echoing back from the chorus, roused Bobby to such a pitch of enthusiasm that he knocked the score off the rail and sent it tumbling down among the rear ranks of the altos.

"Why the unmentionable mischief do you waste your energies, singing like that at a rehearsal?" he demanded abruptly of Thayer, as he joined him on the stairs.

"Where the unmentionable mischief did you come from?" Thayer responded, seizing Bobby's hand in his own firm clasp.

"New York. Just came up, this morning. I'm doing the concert, to-night."

"Oh! I was under the impression that I was going to do a part of it, myself."

"Musically. I represent the power of the Press."

"As critic?"

"Certainly."

"How long since?"

"To-day. The regular critic is busy with a domestic funeral, his grandmother, or step-mother, or something, and it lay between the devil and me to take his place. Strange to say, the Chief chose me; but he was morose enough to say the old lady shouldn't have died, just when all the other papers in town were sending up their best critics."

"But how do you expect to get up a criticism?"

Bobby smiled up at him in smug satisfaction over his own wiliness.

"By caressing the mammon of unrighteousness. I know you; likewise the president of this chorus was in my prep. school. I happened to hear of him, last week, and I am banking on the fact for all it is worth. Therefore I have two strings to my bow. That's more than one of your second violins did. To my certain knowledge, he wrecked two strings in the overture and one in the prelude of your first solo. After that, I got interested and lost count."

"Do you expect us to dictate our own praises?"

"Not much. I am too canny for that. Besides, don't be too sure they will be praises. No; I have asked the president, in strict confidence, just what he thinks of you, and his answer was properly garrulous. His originality was startling, too. He observed that you have temperament. Now I am proceeding to ask you, also in strict confidence, what you think of the chorus."

"That it has intemperament," Thayer responded promptly. "Dane, I abhor that word."

"Is that the reason you coined its negative?"

"No; but it gets on my nerves. When it started out into service, it meant something; but now it is used to express everything, from real artistic feeling down to the way a man rolls up his eyes when he sings love songs. I wish you newspaper men would bring out something new to take its place. You can do it; you generally set the fashion in words."

"I'll ask Lee, when he gets over his funeral," Bobby suggested. "It is out of my line. I am a greater artist than he is, a typographical song without words. I do scareheads, and buffet the devil. Thayer?"

"Yes?"

"Do you honestly enjoy this sort of thing?"

Thayer glanced down at the muddy crossing where they stood waiting for a car to pass.

"No. I prefer an occasional street-cleaning episode; but what can you expect in a March thaw?"

"I don't mean that," Bobby said impatiently. "I'm not joking now."

"Beg pardon," Thayer returned briefly. "What do you mean, Dane?"

"I mean all this tramping round the country, singing to strange people, getting applause at night and reading about yourself, next day. Doesn't it get a frightful bore, after the dozenth time you've been through it?"

"The applause and the audience and the criticisms, yes. The singing, no," Thayer said, after an interval.

"And you're willing to put up with one for the sake of the other?"

"Yes."

Bobby dodged a shower of mud from a passing cab.

"Well, tastes differ, then. In New York, we've been going on the same old routine, and yet no two days have been alike, except in the minor detail of missing you at places. You have been in twenty different cities, and I'd be willing to bet that your routine hasn't varied: sleeper, hotel, rehearsal, concert, applause, wreath, supper, hotel, bed, and so on around the circuit again and again. And you say the singing pays for it. It does pay us; but you can't hear yourself, Thayer, not to get any good of it. If it isn't the applause and such stuff, what do you do it for?"

Thayer glanced down at the man beside him. He liked Bobby Dane, and, for the moment, he felt moved to discard his customary reticence in regard to his art.

"For the sake of feeling myself picked up and carried along by something quite outside myself, something I am powerless to analyze, or to master; yet something that I can help to express," he answered.

Bobby accepted the lesson in silence. Then of a sudden his whimsical fun reasserted itself.

"Must feel a good deal like getting drunk," he commented gravely. "And *à propos des bottes*, Beatrix is at home again."

Thayer's shoulders straightened, his step grew rhythmic once more.

"When did she come?"

"She landed, ten days ago, and they went right to the new house. She is going to send out cards for Mondays in May; but, meanwhile, we are coming in for an earlier event. There's a note at your rooms now, asking you to dine with them, next Monday."

"How do you know?"

"Because, like a coy maiden, I named the day. It is a sort of post-nuptial event, the maid of honor, the best man, and the master of ceremonies, meaning myself. She wasn't going to ask me, because it would spoil the number; but I told her I would make a point of being there, and that Monday was my most convenient day. It will give us our first chance to talk over the wedding."

"How does she--Mrs. Lorimer look?"

"She Mrs. Lorimer looks very natural," Bobby replied gravely. "As a rule, we only say a person looks natural after his demise; but I assure you that Beatrix is very much alive."

"And happy?" Thayer asked involuntarily.

Bobby gave him a swift, sharp glance. Then he resumed his former nonchalant air.

"As happy as one always is at landing after five days of acute sea-sickness. They pursued a storm, all the way home. They didn't catch it, though, except in the figurative sense of our remote childhood. I never saw Beatrix look so happy in her life as when she planted her second foot safely on the pier."

"What about Lorimer?"

Bobby shook his broad shoulders, with the air of a man shaking off a disagreeable subject.

"Oh, he's all right," he said shortly.

Together the two men idled away the afternoon. Bobby would fain have introduced Thayer to his own brother craftsmen who infested the hotel in the hope of getting speech with the artists; but Thayer had little liking for being interviewed, and preferred to divide his time between his own room and the streets. He and Bobby had an apparently limitless fund of talk, and their conversation wandered at will over the events of the past two months. However, as all roads lead to Rome, so all subjects led to Beatrix. When they came around to her in their discussion, Thayer invariably changed the subject; yet even a few words on a constantly recurring theme can end by illuminating that theme perfectly, provided only that it recurs often enough. By the time Thayer was dressing for the concert, that night, he was in full possession of all Bobby Dane's facts concerning his cousin, and he was convinced that all was not well with Lorimer.

With a commendable spirit of originality, the officers of the chorus had broken away from the established rule which proclaimed it an *Elijah* season, and had chosen to give *St. Paul*, that night. Thayer liked the oratorio. It seemed to him more original, more inspired, infinitely more human than the other. Moreover, it would be restful to keep silent and let the tenor warble himself to a lingering death. Even fiery chariots become monotonous in time, and an indignant mob affords a welcome variety. He had not heard the tenor since they had sung together in Berlin, two years before, and he was looking forward to the evening with a good deal of pleasure.

To his surprise and annoyance, he found the music stopping short at his tympani, powerless to enter his brain. When he jolted himself out of his train of subconscious thought, he was aware that the orchestra was superb, that his old friend, the tenor, had added many cubits to his artistic stature, during the past two years, that he himself, Cotton Mather Thayer, would have to use his best efforts if he did not wish to occupy an entirely subordinate place upon the programme. Then he recurred to his thought of Beatrix and Lorimer. If Lorimer had not kept a straight course during his honeymoon, what hope was there for either himself or Beatrix in the many, many moons to come?

The strings and the wind took up the *Allegro*, and Thayer rose. Lorimer, if he had been present, would have known what to expect from the straightening of his shoulders and the sudden squaring of his jaw; but Bobby Dane, who had been watching the apathy in which his friend was buried, was distinctly nervous. Then, at the first note, his nervousness vanished, leaving in its place only wondering admiration. Bobby had supposed he knew what Thayer could do; but he was totally unprepared for the furious dignity with which the singer rendered his aria,--

"Consume them all, Pour out Thine indignation, and let them feel Thy power."

The applause did not wait for the orchestra to slide comfortably back to the tonic. It broke out promptly upon the final note, and it satisfied even Bobby. Thayer bowed his acknowledgments, and then returned to his reverie; but he roused himself again at the *Adagio* which announced his second aria.

Then it was, in Paul's outcry for mercy, for the blotting out of his transgressions, that Bobby Dane understood what Thayer had meant, that noon, when he had spoken of being carried along by something outside of himself. Bobby knew Thayer as a quiet, self-contained man of the world; the Thayer who was singing that great aria was on fire with a passionate madness, tingling with unfulfilled longing, striving against his whole temperament for peace and for pardon. Bobby knew all this; he dimly realized, moreover, that the singer was fired by love for the wife of his friend, burning with the surety that his friend was unworthy of her, and struggling with all the manhood there was in him to face that love and that surety with the stoic calm of one of his Puritan ancestors, to quench the fire and to cover the ashes.

Bobby joined him in the wings, at the close of the concert. Even in the dim light, he could see that Thayer looked whiter than his wont, and that the veins in his temples stood out like knotted cords.

"What business have you to be doing oratorio?" Bobby demanded, as soon as they could struggle a little apart from the gossiping, gushing ranks of the chorus which surrounded them, pulling surreptitious bits from Thayer's mammoth wreath of laurel.

"Why not?" Thayer asked calmly.

"Because you are throwing away the best of yourself. Putting you into oratorio is like icing tea. You belong in grand opera."

Thayer raised his brows dissentingly.

"I wish I could think so, Dane; but I am afraid I should only disappoint you," he answered, and his tone was not altogether jovial, as he said it.

CHAPTER FOURTEEN

"I don't expect to be consistent," Sally retorted. "I'm only an ill-assorted snarl of threads ravelled out from my different ancestors."

"That's dodging the responsibility, Miss Van Osdel."

Bobby lifted an oyster and held it up to view.

"I never did approve of shunting off our sins on the shoulders of our ancestors," he observed. "They sin; we get the come-uppance. You might as well say that the grandfather of this oyster is directly responsible for his being eaten alive."

"No man's sin is wholly his own doing," Lorimer said half bitterly.

There was a sudden pause, as they all came to a realizing sense that Sally's idle words had sent them sliding out upon thin ice. Bobby was the first to rally.

"True for you, Lorimer!" he assented cheerily. "That is one of the doctrines I have spent my life trying to impress on the governor. I wish he felt it more borne in upon him. But, as you were saying, Sally, you're not expecting to become consistent. I'm glad, for you won't be disappointed. The brightest jewel in your crown will have to be of another color."

"What color is consistency, Bobby?" his cousin asked.

"Green, of course, reflected from the jealous eyes of the ninety and nine sinners who haven't the virtue."

"I'm not at all certain that I wish to be consistent," Sally asserted.

"So glad for your sake!" Bobby returned quickly.

Thayer looked up inquiringly.

"Because consistent people are such bores, Miss Van Osdel?"

"So you are a heretic, too? And then they are so smug."

"But there's consistency and consistency," Bobby argued. "There's mashed potato and frappé, for instance, equally hard, equally homogeneous, yet totally different. To my mind, there is a distinct choice between them, and I prefer--"

"Cherries in your frappé." Sally capped his sentence for him. "In other words, we all like a consistent person with lumps of inconsistency. That's myself, and one of my lumps is a dislike of having Mrs. Lloyd Avalons on our tenement committee."

"But, if you are slumming--"

"That is ignoble of you, Beatrix. The committee doesn't slum within its own confines."

"Oh, I didn't mean that at all," Beatrix protested hastily. "Really, though. I can't see why you and Mrs. Lloyd Avalons can't unite in working for somebody quite outside either of your worlds."

Sally raised her brows in saucy imitation of Mrs. Lloyd Avalons's pet expression. Then she pushed Beatrix's words aside with daintily outstretched fingers.

"Can't you?" she said coolly, as she ended her little pantomime. "Well, I can. To adopt Bobby's choice illustration, it would be like mixing potato and frappé. The potato would melt the frappé, and then the frappé would--well, would render the potato unpalatable. In other words, if we work together, I shall pulverize Mrs. Lloyd Avalons, and then the dust of her individuality will get in among my nerves and clog them."

"If you can't be consistent, Miss Van Osdel, please do try to be concrete," Thayer urged. "I confess that I find it a little difficult to follow you."

"Not at all," Bobby interposed. "She isn't going anywhere. Sally's mental processes always remind me of the way we used to play cars in a row of easy chairs. We were extremely energetic, and we pretended that we were going somewhere; but in reality we didn't budge an inch. Sally, what is the reason you don't like Mrs. Lloyd Avalons?"

"Because she is utterly preposterous," Sally replied concisely.

"And yet, she is bound to arrive, some day," Lorimer said thoughtfully.

"Then I hope it may not be until after I have left," Sally retorted. "I don't care to have her making connections with me."

"Sally, you are uncharitable," Beatrix said rebukingly; but Bobby interrupted,--

"That's more than you can say of Mrs. Lloyd Avalons. She is on half the charity committees in town."

"How did she get there?" Thayer asked, with unfeigned curiosity.

"By toiling upward, day and night. That's where she scores ahead of the great men. According to the poet, they only belonged to the night shift. Mrs. Lloyd Avalons sleeps with the Blue Book under her pillow and dreams social combinations."

"She probably has a chess board always at her elbow," Sally suggested. "I can fancy the game, the white queen and her pawn against the whole black force, each man neatly tagged with his name and social status."

"She is marching straight into the king-row, though," Bobby added.

Beatrix called them to order.

"Does it strike you that this is perilously near to being gossip?" she inquired.

But Sally had the last word.

"It's not gossip to talk over the possibilities of the lower classes," she remarked imperturbably. "It is social science."

Lorimer went back to the original question which had started the discussion.

"As I said before, there is a certain inconsistency in the idea of a given number of women setting themselves to work to better the condition of the masses, and then coming to wreck and ruin because one of their number is of a slightly different set."

"Slightly inferior," Sally corrected him.

Lorimer accepted the amendment.

"Inferior, then, if you choose. But we are talking of the theory in the abstract, not of any particular case. One hardly expects to find snobbishness in slumming."

"Then that's where one gets left," Bobby commented, by way of parenthesis.

"But if you are all stooping?"

"Yes; but the alignment is better, if we all stoop at the same angle," Sally protested.

"What I wish to know," Thayer said thoughtfully; "is where the deadline of propriety exists. Take the case of Mrs. Lloyd Avalons, for instance. Why does she take Patsey Keefe to her heart and home, and snub Arlt upon all occasions?"

"Because she wishes to maintain a proper perspective," Sally replied. "Everyone knows that Patsey and she are chums from choice; with Mr. Arlt, there might be a question. Legitimate slumming presupposes two willing parties, the slummer and the slummed."

"In other words," Bobby added; "it is socially possible to foregather with the slum in the next ward; it is death to speak to the undesirable neighbor in the back alley. The fact is ordained; but it will take several generations of social scientists to ferret out the cause."

Sally addressed the table at large.

"For my part, I like Mr. Arlt," she said flatly. "What's more, I am going with him to the Kneisel concert, to-morrow night; and, if any of you are there and choose to eye me askance, you are welcome."

Later, that evening, Thayer found himself with Beatrix and a little apart from the others. The dinner had been utterly informal, and it had been tacitly understood that the guests should linger afterwards. It was only ten days since the Lorimers had landed from their European honeymoon, and as yet they felt themselves privileged to hold themselves a little aloof from the social treadmill. Though the breakfast table, each morning, was littered with cards and notes of invitation, yet the season was in their favor. Lent had entered upon its last week, and even the largest functions clothed themselves in penitential and becoming shades of violet. Accordingly, it had been a source of little self-denial for Bobby and Sally to give up their other engagements for the evening. As for Thayer, he invariably went his own way, invited everywhere and appearing only in the places which suited his mood of the hour. It was the one professional luxury that he allowed himself.

To his keen eye, Beatrix looked as if she were carrying a heavy burden of care. She was as alert as ever; her social training was bound to ensure that. But between her conversational sallies, her face settled into certain fixed lines that were new to Thayer. Even during the past two months, her lips had grown firmer; but her lids drooped more often, as if to hide some secret which otherwise might be betrayed by her eyes. Up to this time, Thayer had never called her especially pretty. She was handsome, perhaps; but her face was too cold, too austere. Now, however, it seemed to him full of possibilities for beauty, softer, infinitely more loving. In the old days, the curve of her lips had been haughty; to-night, their firmer lines appeared to him like a mask worn to conceal the gentler womanhood within. She was thinner, too; but browned by her sea voyage, and she carried herself with the nameless dignity which comes to a woman upon her bridal day.

Lorimer appeared to be in the pink of condition. He was more handsome than ever, more graciously winning. His voice had all the old caressing intonations which Thayer recalled so well, together with many new ones that crept into his tone whenever he addressed his wife. By look and word and gesture, he referred and deferred to her constantly; and his eyes never failed to light, when they rested upon her own. No man could have been more frankly and openly in love with his own wife.

"Then I take it for granted that the trip has been a success," Thayer said, as he joined her.

"Indeed it has. Mr. Lorimer took me to all his old haunts and, in Berlin, to all of yours that he could find. We went to your old lodgings, and we heard a concert in the hall where you made your début and, the last day we were there, Sidney insisted upon hunting up your old master."

Thayer looked up suddenly.

"The dear old *Maestro*! Did he remember me?" he asked, with a boyish enthusiasm which sat well upon him.

"Certainly he did, if *remember* is the right word, for his knowledge of you was not all in the past tense. He has followed you closely, and he knows just what you have done. Mr. Thayer," she added abruptly; "why have you never sung in opera?"

"Why should I?"

"Because he said that there was your especial talent, only he called it by a stronger name. He jeers at the work you are doing."

Thayer smiled.

"I am sorry. I thought it was good work."

"So it is, as far as it goes. But the other goes farther."

"Perhaps," he assented. "But do you think it is as--as--"

"Good form?" she queried, laughing. "Yes, if you choose to have it so. It depends something upon the individual. With your training and traditions, you would scarcely elect to sing comic opera in English."

"Heaven forbid!" he said hastily. "But there are grades and grades, even of the other. Not many mortals reach the top round of the ladder."

"No; and, even if they did, they would be a good deal in your way, for the space up there is limited. It will be merely a question of your own will whether or not you occupy a part of it."

He was surprised at the turn the conversation had taken. No woman, not even Miss Gannion, had ever dared question to him the wisdom of his choice, or imply to him that there were laurels which he had not yet plucked. Strange to say, he rather enjoyed the frank fashion in which Beatrix was taking him to task. Nevertheless, he fenced a little.

"I have always preferred a moderate success to an immoderate failure," he answered her.

She shook her head.

"That sounds specious; but you know it is a quibble. I had never supposed that your ambition was so limited."

"But it is not the mark of limitation to know where my success lies."

"Perhaps not. For my part, though, I don't want to rest on any success. If I succeed in one thing, that is over and done with, and I want to try for something else."

"And if you fail?"

"Then, as soon as I am quite sure it is a failure and that no power of mine can beat it into a success, I try to turn my back upon it, and face another problem," she replied, with a quiet dignity which ignored the flush that rose in both their faces at the careless question.

Thayer, too, had seen the flush in her cheeks which had answered to his own rising color. For an instant, he questioned whether it were an unwitting acknowledgment that her power over Lorimer was more limited than she had supposed. Then he dismissed the suspicion. Her poise was too perfect to make such a supposition possible. It was only that he, knowing the truth, sought for confirmation upon all sides.

"You are a good fighter," he responded quietly. "What would be the concrete application of your theory to my practice?"

"That you should try to fulfil the ambition your old master has for you," she returned. "Why don't you try it? You can't gain any more glory in your present field; you stand at the head of concert and oratorio singers in America. You have nothing to lose; and, over there in Berlin, there is an old man who boasts that he made your voice, and says that he can never sing his *Nunc Dimittis* until you have entered upon your right path."

Thayer's face softened.

"Did he say that?"

"Yes, and he extorted a promise from me that I would tell you his very words. That is the reason I have made bold to speak about the matter."

"What do you think about it, yourself, Mrs. Lorimer?"

"That he knows your possibilities much better than I," she answered evasively.

"But you have an opinion," he urged.

"Yes, I have," she replied frankly. "From what he told me, and from what I have heard of your singing, I know that you can do broader work than any you have attempted. Your voice will do for either thing, opera or oratorio; but on a few times--" she hesitated; then she went on without flinching; "on the night of the Fresh Air Fund concert, for instance, you showed a dramatic power that is wasted in your present work." Suddenly she laughed at her own earnestness. "What am I, that I should advise the star of the season? Do excuse my frankness, Mr. Thayer."

"I asked you."

"That's no reason I should bore you with all my theories upon a subject of which I know practically nothing. And, meanwhile, I am forgetting to tell you that we went to see Frau Arlt."

His face showed his pleasure and his approval, his pleasure that he had found something in Lorimer to which he could give his unreserved approval.

"I am glad you saw her. It was like Lorimer to hunt her up. Does Otto know about it?"

"He came to dinner, a day or two after we landed. Mr. Lorimer had written him a note to tell him we were at home, and you should have seen the boy's delight over the box of funny little odds and ends his mother had sent him. Sidney is always so thoughtful, and he suggested to the old lady that we had room in our trunks for a package. I really think that the boy was happier with his home-made gifts than I was with the things Mr. Lorimer gave me in Paris."

[Illustration: "It was so that Thayer liked best to think of her"]

"He has been a very brave, but a very homesick little German," Thayer answered, while his eyes rested thoughtfully on her face. It brightened now, as she spoke of Lorimer, and a half-tender, half-amused smile was playing around her lips. All in all, Thayer was broad enough to like it better so.

Suddenly she rose, as if to end their conversation; but she turned back again to add,--

"Of all my wedding gifts, Mr. Thayer, the sweetest was the blessing of good old Frau Arlt. She will never forget Mr. Lorimer, and her story of his kindness in their darkest days, her good wishes to me, and her happiness in seeing us will always stand out as an unforgettable picture. You knew all about it, of course; but I had no idea how good to them Sidney had been, nor how full of tact."

The smile still lingered about her lips, and her cheeks were flushed a little, as she turned away in answer to her husband's call. For long months to come, it was so that Thayer liked best to think of her.

CHAPTER FIFTEEN

Beatrix raised her eyes from her letters. "Mother wants us to come to dinner, to-night, Sidney."

"But you are scheduled for something else; aren't you?" he answered, without looking up from his paper.

"For nothing that I can't break. There are some teas and the theatre. I had thought I might have to hurry our dinner, to get through in time. What if we give up the theatre? The Andersons won't mind, if we telephone them so early."

"Just as well," he responded indifferently, as he turned his paper inside out and ran his eye down the columns.

"Then shall I telephone mother that we will be there?"

"You can go, Beatrix. I sha'n't be able to be there."

"Why not, Sidney?"

"Because Dudley is giving a dinner at the club, to-night, and I am booked for that."

"Oh, Sidney!" She checked herself abruptly.

Lowering his paper, he looked at her in surprise.

"What is it, dear?" he asked.

"Nothing, only--I wouldn't go."

"But I can't get out of it. Dudley made a point of my being there, and I told him to count on me."

"I am sorry," she said quietly. "I don't like Mr. Dudley."

"Neither do I especially. Still, I saw a good deal of him at one time, and, to-night, he wants to get together the old set. It's sort of a farewell spread, for he starts for Nome, next week."

"But you had promised the Andersons."

"Yes, I told Anderson that I would get around in time to mingle my tears with yours over the fifth act. Anderson is such a bore that I couldn't stand a whole evening of him."

"Then I shall certainly refuse to go," Beatrix said decidedly.

Lorimer raised his brows inquiringly.

"For any especial reason?"

She had risen from the table, and now she stood looking down at him, a world of disappointed love showing in her dark eyes. She forced herself to smile a little, as her eyes met his.

"I am old-fashioned, Sidney. I don't like going to the theatre with other men than my husband, four months after my wedding day."

He dropped his paper hastily, and, rising, linked his arm in hers.

"Why, Beatrix dear, I didn't suppose--"

"No," she said quietly; "but I wish you had supposed. Still, as long as I found it out in time, there is no great harm done."

"But with older people like the Andersons," he urged. "And I should have been there to come home with you."

She was silent, and he went on, after a pause,--

"I didn't think of your minding, dear girl. You know that I wouldn't be discourteous to you for anything."

"Never mind about it now, Sidney. I can telephone to Mrs. Anderson, and it will be all right," she answered more gently, for she felt the contrition in his tone and it softened her momentary resentment at his calm way of adjusting her convenience and happiness to his plans. "Mother said Bobby is coming, and possibly Sally Van Osdel. She wanted the four of us to go there for an impromptu dinner such as we used to have."

"I am sorry, dear." There was a real note of regret in Lorimer's voice. "She should have telephoned us earlier."

"She waited for Bobby's decision. He is the only one of us, you know, who makes even a pretence of being busy. Besides, as late in the season as this, it is generally safe to count on people."

"Apparently not," Lorimer returned lightly. "At least, I seem to be the unlucky exception that proves the rule. I am sorry, for I know your mother's dinners of old. I would break most engagements for them."

"Why not this?" she urged.

"Impossible. I promised, a week ago."

Her face flushed.

"How does it happen you haven't mentioned it?"

His answering laugh was frank and free from any taint of bitterness.

"Because I knew you didn't like Dudley, dear girl, and I didn't see any use in discussing a matter on which we were bound to differ." He evidently had had no intention of saying more; but, as he saw her downcast face, he went on, "Truly, Beatrix, I couldn't decently refuse the fellow, without any good reason."

She raised her eyes to his face a little haughtily.

"But it seems to me you had a good reason."

Lorimer laughed again. It was plain that he was determined not to be jarred out of his genial mood.

"A good reason; but not one that was very tellable. You really don't want me saying to a man that I can't eat his dinner because my wife dislikes him."

Lorimer had no notion that his words could sting his wife, and he was surprised at her heightened color and at the sudden aggressive poise of her head. Then swiftly she controlled herself.

"Next time, you can concoct some more specious reason," she answered, with forced lightness.

In his turn, Lorimer felt himself irritated by her calm feminine assumption that his acceptance or refusal of invitations in future was to be bounded by her dislikes.

"Next time, we will hope you will have annulled the reason," he retorted. "Dudley isn't a bad fellow. Moreover, he has the saving grace of knowing how to order a good dinner and get together a good crowd."

She felt the half-veiled hostility of his tone, and it cut her. She had received similar cuts before, during the past three or four months. Instead of rendering her callous, they had left a sore sensitiveness in their scars. She battled against the soreness bravely. The Danes were a race with level nerves, trained by generations of self-control to look upon moods and lack of breeding as synonymous terms; and Beatrix had had no conception of the swift alternations of feeling which marked and marred the temperament of Lorimer. Often as they had been together during their rather long engagement, he had been able to maintain a moderately even mood whenever Beatrix was within reach. On one or two occasions, he had betrayed the fact that he was gloomy and depressed; but it was not until they came into the every-day and all-day contact which follows upon the heels of the marriage ceremony that she had supposed he could be either irritable or petulant. By the time they had come home from Europe, she was quite aware of both characteristics; yet they were alternated with hours of passionate devotion, of a tender chivalry which took away much of their sting. Lorimer loved his wife loyally; nevertheless, the very traits which most won the admiration of his better hours, were the first ones to antagonize him when his moments of irritation were upon him.

If Beatrix had been of the same temper, the danger for the future would have been infinitely less. Flash would have answered to flash; and then the quiet current would have run on as if the perfect contact had never been broken. Instead of that, her quieter, better-controlled nature received his flashes and made no outward sign of the shock. In the end, she remained painfully sensitive to his petulance, while his real love for her left her unbelieving, cold and apathetic. She had proof of the one; the other was mainly negative, in so far as practical results were concerned.

"Who are to be there?" she asked, as soon as she could trust her voice to be properly inexpressive.

"Austin, and Tom Forbes, and Lloyd Avalons, and two or three men you don't know, and Thayer."

"Mr. Thayer?" Her accent was incredulous.

"Certainly. Why not?"

"I didn't know that he ever had anything to do with Mr. Dudley, and I really can't imagine his caring to make a table companion of Lloyd Avalons."

Lorimer's answering laugh was slightly bitter.

"What a social Philistine you are, Beatrix! Thayer is not so narrow."

"Does that mean I am narrow?" she asked resentfully.

"Yes, for a woman who frowned disapproval upon Sally Van Osdel's late utterances."

"Sally was talking of Mrs. Lloyd Avalons. Mrs. Lloyd Avalons is not bad, only foolish: Mr. Lloyd Avalons is both." She drew a long breath, as she paused with her teeth shut upon her lower lip. Suddenly her chin began to quiver, and two heavy tears slid down her cheeks. Then she rallied swiftly, for she knew that all men hate domestic tears. "Sidney," she said slowly and with an evident effort towards steadiness; "let's not discuss this any more. I will go to mother's, and you may come for me there, after your dinner is over. I wish you could go with me; but never mind. Only, Sidney,--next time, please tell me a little sooner when you make a dinner engagement, and then I shall know just how to fit my plans into yours. And--?" She raised her eyes to meet his squarely.

He understood.

"Yes, dear girl, I will be careful," he said, as he drew her to his side.

For a moment, she stood there, passive. Then she went away out of the room.

Thayer was the last guest to arrive, that night, and when he entered the room, he found that both host and *chef* were anxiously awaiting his coming. He had spent the past two hours with Arlt, listening to scraps of the completed overture, suggesting, praising, criticising it with an acumen which surprised even the young composer, though he was fast learning to attribute omniscience to his friend. After the shabby room with its half-light, after the intent earnestness of Arlt, Thayer felt a passing dislike of the gorgeousness and glare and frivolity of the dinner. He was the last man to assert that good art can only associate itself with homely origins, that prosperity is a deadly foe to its growth. Nevertheless, he was fully conscious that Arlt in his meagre surroundings was much nearer to his own ideals than were the immaculate guests of the evening. Thayer loved luxury; but it must not be accompanied by empty-headedness.

Thayer had had a definite purpose in accepting his invitation, that night, a purpose which was quite alien to his mental estimate of his host. Dudley, to his mind, was in some respects a shade or two better than Lloyd Avalons, yet many shades worse in that his caddishness came from deliberate choice, not from lack of training. In any case, Thayer prayed that he might be remote from either of them, at table.

He quickly discovered that his prayer had been unavailing. He found himself at the host's right hand, with Lorimer directly opposite. Lloyd Avalons was next to Lorimer, and, as the dinner progressed by easy stages, Thayer became aware that his purpose in coming was about to be put to the test. The dinner was good and abundant; the wines were better and yet more abundant, and Lloyd Avalons, who appeared to be constructed of some material which alcohol was powerless to attack, saw to it that Lorimer's glass was filled as often as his own. The result was inevitable. Before Lloyd Avalons felt the slightest exhilaration, Lorimer's brown cheeks were stained with red, and his voice was mounting by semitones, then by whole tones, while his accent took on a curiously insistent note which was quite foreign to the trivial subjects of discussion.

"How did it happen that you were at Eton, Lorimer?" Dudley asked, at the end of an unnecessarily long story.

"My father took me over. He was at St. James, you know, and he thought I would find more fellows of my own class at Eton than up here at Andover."

"That's modest of you, Lorimer," someone called, from the foot of the table. "But please remember that I'm an Andover man."

"And even then wouldn't they accept you for the ministry?" Lorimer asked promptly.

The man laughed with perfect good-temper. Already he was two glasses ahead of Lorimer; but no outward sign betrayed the fact.

"I am willing to bet that they kept you more strict at Eton than the Doctor kept us."

Lorimer set down his glass and gave a knowing wink which, at another time, he would have been swift to condemn in his left-hand neighbor.

"They tried; but they couldn' do much about it. Besides, there was college, you know."

"We all have experienced university discipline," Dudley suggested. "It is swift and powerful, and nobody ever knows where it will hit next."

Lorimer appeared to be pondering the matter. Then he turned to Lloyd Avalons.

"D' you ever 'sperience university discipline?" he demanded, with grave anxiety.

Lloyd Avalons flushed angrily, and Thayer judged that it was time to interpose.

"University discipline is more a matter of theory than of fact," he said lightly. "If you want real discipline, you'd better go through a course of voice training. How much was my allowance, the last of the time in Berlin, Lorimer? My salamanders were mere tadpoles."

Lorimer caught at the familiar word.

"*Ein! Zwei! Drei! Salamander! Salamander! Salamander!*" he cried gayly. "It makesh me homesick for the good ol' days in Berlin."

"You were over, in January; weren't you?" Lloyd Avalons asked.

"Yes, aft' a fashion; but 't wasn' the ol' fashion. A studen' an' a married man's two differen' things. I took Mrs. Lorimer everywhere an' to show her grat'tude she took me in han'." And Lorimer's own laugh rang out merrily at what seemed to him a superlatively good joke.

The next moment, Thayer's level voice, low, yet so perfectly trained that it reached the farthest corner of the room, broke in upon Lorimer's mirth and quenched it. There was no bitterness in his voice, no excitement; he spoke as quietly as if he had been wishing his friend good-morning.

"It's a pity she isn't here to take you in hand now, Lorimer," he said, with a smile. "As long as she isn't, I think perhaps I'll do it, myself."

The deliberate, even tone steadied Lorimer somewhat. He pulled himself together and stared haughtily at Thayer.

"What do you mean?" he demanded. "I don't understand you."

There was a short silence while it pleased Lorimer to imagine that he was measuring his puny strength against the power of the other. Then, before Thayer's gray eyes, his own eyes drooped.

"I think you do understand, Lorimer," Thayer said calmly. "If not, we can talk it over outside. You know we are due at Mrs. Dane's at ten, and it is almost that, now. Dudley, I am sorry that this is good-by for so long. Don't let us break up the party." And, rising, he nodded to the other guests and took his departure without a backward glance.

He had reckoned accurately, for experience had taught him to know his man. Lorimer sat still for a moment, then hesitated, and rose. He bade an over-cordial good-night to Dudley and Lloyd Avalons, exchanged with the others a jesting word or two of which the humor was obviously forced; then he sullenly followed Thayer out of the room and out of the club.

Once safely in the street, Thayer freed his mind, forcibly and tersely according to his wont.

"It's bad enough to fall into temptation, Lorimer; but the fellow who deliberately canters into it comes mighty near not being worth the saving. Some day, you'll wake up to find the truth of that fact; and then Heaven help you, for there may not be anyone else willing to take the trouble!"

CHAPTER SIXTEEN

Slowly and by almost imperceptible stages, spring had crept into summer and summer had crawled sluggishly into autumn. Rose color had turned to green, green to gold, and then all colors had faded to the uniform gray of November. To Beatrix it seemed that nature's change typified that of her life; to Thayer and Arlt the rose color and the gold were still glowing. For the time being, the problems of their professional lives were absorbing them both, to the exclusion of more human interests. Such epochs are bound to come to every man. However broad and generous-minded he may be, there are hours when it seems to him that the rising of the sun and the going down of the same are functions of nature ordained merely for the sake of giving chronological record of his own professional advancement. November brought them both to this mood and, while it lasted, each found the other his only satisfactory companion.

To Thayer the summer had been a matter of personal mathematics, the solving of simultaneous personal equations. He had refused the Lorimers' urgent invitation to join them at Monomoy. He had felt unequal to prolong the double strain he had endured, those last weeks in town before society broke up for the summer. It was almost unbearable to him to be within daily reach of Beatrix, to be forced to face her with the unvarying conventional smile of mere social acquaintance. It was infinitely worse to be forced to look on and watch the gradual wrecking of her hopes, to know that she was unhappy, discouraged and full of fear for the future, and to realize that another man was carelessly bringing upon her all this from which he would have given his own life to shield her. Yet bad and worse were subordinated to worst. The worst, the most unbearable phase of the whole situation lay in the knowledge, again and again brought to the proof, that he himself was the only living person who had the ability to hold Lorimer even approximately steady, that in a way the thread of his destiny was knotted together with that of Beatrix. He loved her absolutely, and the only proof of his love for her must lie in his strange power to make more tolerable for her the galling yoke of her marriage to another man.

Even in these few short months, it had become evident to the world that the yoke was a galling one. Beatrix wore it bravely, even haughtily. Nevertheless, it was chafing her until she was raw. Like a horse surprised by the discovery of its own power, from occasional friskiness, Lorimer was settling into a steadily increasing pace. During the months of probation, he had held himself fairly steady, rather than lose the chance of winning Beatrix for his wife. Now that she was won, he snapped the check he had put upon himself, and yielded to the acquired momentum gained during his self-imposed repression. By the time he came home from Europe, Bobby and Thayer both realized that something was amiss. By the first of June, it was an open secret that all was not well with Lorimer's soul.

Lorimer still loved Beatrix with all the fervor of his nature. To him, she was the one and only woman in the world, someone to be caressed and indulged and played with, the comrade of his domestic hours. But, when the other mood was upon him, he acknowledged no right upon her part to offer advice or warning. He treated her as one treats a spoiled child, fondling her until her presence bored him or interfered with his other plans, then quietly setting her aside and going his own way alone. As far as any woman could have held him, Beatrix could have done so; but in Lorimer's life feminine influence was finite. When he was moved to take the bits in his teeth, only a man, and but one man at that, was able to check him. That man was Cotton Mather Thayer.

On a few occasions, Beatrix had endeavored to hold her husband, not from temptation itself, but from the first steps towards it. She might as well have tried to bar the rising tide with a pint sieve. At such times, it seemed to her that Lorimer deliberately made up his mind to have a revel, that he set himself to work to carry out his desires to a satisfactory conclusion. These periods came at irregular intervals; but, all in all, the intervals were shortening and the revels were increasing. Beatrix learned their symptoms far too quickly; she learned to know the depression and irritability which greeted her every effort to rouse and to please him. It was at such times that Lorimer made bitter revolt against what he termed her narrowness and prejudice, or burst into occasional angry petulance, if she tried to urge him to cut loose from the club and from the constantly-growing influence of Lloyd Avalons who was discerning enough to discover that Lorimers appetite was a possible lever by which he himself might pry himself up into a more stable position in society. In this matter, however, Lloyd Avalons was not quite so unprincipled as he seemed. To his mind, there was nothing so very bad about a little matter of social intoxication. The evil of drink was an affair bounded by purely geographical lines, and he encouraged in Lorimer the very thing for which he would have been prompt to dismiss the man who cleaned the snow off his sidewalk.

Afterwards, when the depression had ended in the revel, when they both had ended in penitence, Lorimer temporarily came back again to the old ways. The caressing intonations returned to his voice, as he talked to Beatrix; his eyes followed her with loving pride, as she moved about the room; for days at a time he devoted himself to her wishes, serving her with a tireless chivalry which made her long to forget all that had gone before. However, Beatrix could not forget certain facts; certain episodes were so fixed in her memory that they seemed branded upon the very tissue of her life. In some respects, these intervening days were the hardest ones she had to bear. Lorimer seemed totally unable to grasp the fact that any permanent barrier was rising between them, that there was any real reason why they should not meet on precisely the old ground. To his mind, half an hour of impulsive penitence could wipe out half a night of deliberate sin, and Beatrix dared not explain to him that it was otherwise. Her hold over him, that hold which once she had deemed so strong, was growing slighter with every passing month. Any hasty or ill-considered word from her might have the effect of destroying it altogether. For the present, the most she could do, was to avoid antagonizing him; and even that was no easy task. She was quite unable to decide whether it took more self-control to accept in silence his petulance or his caresses. Meanwhile, she was thankful for the apparently growing friendship between Thayer and her husband. During late May and all of June, Thayer was with Lorimer almost daily, and Lorimer came nearest to his old, winning self on the days when he had been longest in company with Thayer.

With the general scattering of people which heralds the coming of summer, it seemed to Thayer that, for the time being, Lorimer's danger was over, and it was with a sigh of utter relief that he saw Lorimer and Beatrix starting for Monomoy. Strong as he was, Thayer had felt the strain of the past six weeks; and it was good to hide himself with Arlt in a Canadian fishing village, dismiss his responsibilities to his neighbor, and give himself up to absolute idleness and much good music.

He had planned to spend August and September in Germany; but fate willed otherwise. Less than a week before he was to sail, he received a laconic epistle from Bobby Dane, dated at the hotel where he himself had spent the previous summer.

"DEAR THAYER,--Wish you could come down here for August. Lorimer is raising the deuce, and I can't do much with him. Besides, I am ordered back, next week. I suppose the devil needs my ministrations. I'll see to one, if you'll tackle the other.

Yours, R. F. DANE."

Thayer hesitated for three minutes. Then he wrote two telegrams. One was to the office of the steamship company. The other was to the hotel near Monomoy.

The reaction which followed, was a natural one. Late in September, Thayer returned to New York, preparatory to a concert tour through New England. Exhausted by the long strain of mastering both himself and Lorimer, he threw himself into his work with a feverish intensity which astounded Arlt and roused his audiences to the highest pitch of enthusiasm. Thayer took his new honors quietly, however. In his secret heart, he knew that this had been the simplest way to work off his stored-up emotions, and he reached New York, early in November, with a greater reputation and steadier nerves than he had even dared to hope.

The tour had been a prosperous one for Arlt, as well. Upon several occasions, he had met with marked favor, and the little touch of success had reacted upon his personality, rendering him more at ease, more masterful with his audience. To be popular, art must be modest; but woe betide it, if it be in the least deprecating! However, Arlt was learning to face his public with a fairly good grace, and his public showed itself willing to smile back at him in a thoroughly friendly fashion.

Arlt's overture was to have its first hearing, the week before Thanksgiving. The matter had been arranged through the influence of his teacher, and Arlt had been invited to conduct the orchestra for the event. However, in spite of his added ease, Arlt had judged such an ordeal too great for his courage. Accordingly, the teacher and Thayer had taken council together, with the result that Thayer was engaged as soloist for the evening, and that Thayer insisted upon singing one group of songs with a piano accompaniment. To this minor detail, Arlt had been forced to submit, although he was shrewd enough to see that it was merely a ruse on the part of his teacher to bring him in person before his audience.

The arrangement of these details, the orchestral rehearsals of the overture and his own rehearsals with Arlt were engrossing Thayer completely. Heart and soul, he was working for the boy's success, for he realized that into this simple overture Arlt had put the very best of himself, that the young composer's happiness was bound up in the success or failure of his maiden effort. The creative power had come upon him; he had worked to the utmost limit with the material ready to his brain. Now he was waiting to have the world pass judgment whether his work was worth the doing, whether he should keep on, or turn his back upon his chosen path. Thayer's own plans, too, were maturing. In the watching them develop, in the helping Arlt to pass the time of waiting, he almost succeeded in forgetting the Lorimers. Almost; but not quite. The forgetting was a little too intentional to be entirely complete. He met them rarely. Society had not yet organized its winter campaign, and it was still possible for a man to go his own individual way. Just now, Thayer's own individual way led him almost daily in the direction of Washington Square.

He was in Arlt's room, one evening, less than a week before the concert. He had been dining with Miss Gannion; but he had left her early, in order to impress upon Arlt that he must accept his bidding to the supper which the Lorimers were to give after the concert. The invitations had been noncommittal, and Arlt had announced his intention of declining his own, on the plea of being too tired with his overture to care to do anything more, that night. Miss Gannion had told Thayer what he already half suspected, that Beatrix was really giving this supper in Arlt's honor and that it was to be the first large affair of the season, in the hope of focussing public attention upon the boy at the very moment of his having proved his real genius as composer.

Thayer appreciated to the full the gracious kindliness of the plan, and he had excused himself to Miss Gannion and hurried away in search of Arlt, devoutly praying, as he went, that the note of regret might not be already on its way.

He was but just in time. The sealed note lay on the table, and Arlt was shrugging himself into his overcoat, when Thayer entered the room. Ten minutes later, they were still arguing the matter, when they heard an unfamiliar step coming up the stairs.

"Mr. Arlt?" A strange voice followed the knock.

Arlt opened the door hospitably. The dim light in the hallway showed him a figure known to every opera singer in America and half of Europe.

"Will you come in?" he asked, in some surprise.

"Is Mr. Thayer here?"

"I am." Thayer stepped into the lighted doorway. "You wished me?"

"Yes. What is more, I need you. We know each other well by sight, so I suppose there is no call for us to waste time on introductions. Mr. Thayer, Principali, one of my best baritones, is ill and is forced to cancel his engagements. Will you take his place?"

Thayer meditated swiftly, during a moment of silence.

"What are the operas?"

"Wagner, *Faust* of course, and--oh, the usual run of extras."

"What reason have you to think that I am fitted for your vacancy?" Thayer asked directly.

The impresario smiled.

"Your old master in Berlin is one of my most intimate friends. He gave you a letter of introduction to me, I think?" The accent was interrogative, although it was plain that only one answer was expected.

"He did," Thayer assented quietly.

"Yes, and I have been waiting for more than a year in the hope that you would present it. Since you will not come to me, I am at last driven to go in search of you."

Thayer bowed gravely in recognition of the implied compliment. He realized that he was suddenly facing a question which might affect his whole after life, and he was too much in earnest to waste words on mere conventional phrases. He liked the old man, and he felt a swift, burning longing to accept his offer. It had come unsought, unexpected. Was not fate in it; and was not a man always justified in following out his fate? To accept it would be in a great measure to cut himself off from his present social life. An operatic engagement would engross him completely. All in all, it might be better so. And yet, there was something to be said upon the other side. Was he justified in working out his own professional salvation at the certain cost of the damnation of another soul? That was what it amounted to in the long run. If he went into opera, he must separate himself from all connection with Sidney Lorimer. He could not take the time to visit Lorimer's world; it would be sure and swift destruction to Lorimer, if he were to set foot within the new world which Thayer was preparing to enter. Thayer realized that the horns of his dilemma were long and curving. The offer tempted him sorely; yet, for some unaccountable reason, he shrank from turning his back upon Lorimer. And, besides, if Beatrix--

"How long would you need me?"

"The entire season."

"How soon?"

"In *Faust*, on the tenth of next month."

"In *Faust*?"

The impresario saw that Thayer was hesitating. The idea of Faust plainly attracted him, and the impresario hastily followed up the advantage.

"Yes, we want you for *Valentine*."

"My favorite part," Thayer said, half to himself.

The impresario smiled serenely. He felt no question now as to the outcome of his errand.

"Calvé will sing *Marguerite*; it will be a good cast. After that, we shall need you, two or three times a week, and the salary--"

Impatiently Thayer brushed his words aside.

"How soon must you have my answer?"

"To-night."

"Very well. Then, no."

The impresario straightened up in his chair.

"Mr. Thayer!" he remonstrated.

"It is impossible for me to bind myself for an entire season, without more time to think the matter over," Thayer said quietly.

"But it is important that I should know, in order to make my other arrangements."

"Then you would better consider it settled in the negative," Thayer returned.

The impresario wavered.

"How much time do you need?" he asked a little impatiently.

"I must have a week."

"Impossible."

"Very well, then. But I thank you for the honor you have done me in asking me to fill the place."

Thayer rose with an air of decision, and the impresario could do nothing else than follow his example. At the door, he turned back.

"Mr. Thayer, there is no use in my trying to conceal the fact that I want you badly. If I will wait until a week from to-night, will you give me your answer then?"

"I will," Thayer replied imperturbably.

"And sign the contracts on the spot?"

"I will," Thayer repeated; "but remember this: in the meantime, I am binding myself to nothing. Good-night."

He went down the stairs with the impresario. When he returned to Arlt's room, a moment later, he took up the conversation at the precise point where they had dropped it; but, even in the dusky room, Arlt could see that Thayer's eyes were blazing as he had never seen them till then. Not long afterwards, Thayer glanced down at his own strong, slim hand that rested on the table beside him. The fingers were moving restlessly and, on the back, the cords twitched a little now and then. Thayer watched it curiously for a moment. Then he clasped his hands on his knee and held them there, motionless.

CHAPTER SEVENTEEN

Above the murmur of talk of his guests, Lorimer's voice rose, high and clear, merry as the voice of a happy child.

"It's a great night for you, Arlt, the night of your life. Ladies and ge'men, le's drink to Mr. Arlt."

"You've done it once, Lorimer," Thayer interposed. "Arlt will be getting more than is good for him."

"And so will you," he might have added; but there seemed to him a certain impossibility in imposing a check upon a man in his own house and in the presence of his own guests.

Lorimer laughed out blithely.

"Ne' mind. Arlt can stand it; his head is level. B'sides, las' time, I drank to Arlt the composer. This time, it's to Arlt the accompanist. He hasn' any business to play a double rôle, if he can' stan' the double applause. To the success of Mr. Otto Arlt!"

Thayer raised his glass and set it down again, untasted. As he glanced across at Arlt with an explanatory smile, he caught the eyes of Beatrix fixed upon him imploringly. It was evident that she was putting her hope in him to end the scene; but for the once Thayer was ready to confess himself beaten. The house and the champagne both were Lorimer's. Under these conditions, he was powerless to act. Moreover, he felt a sudden impatience with Beatrix for allowing the champagne in her own home, when she had learned from months of bitter experience that a single glass could render Lorimer totally untrustworthy. If this were the measure of her influence for good, she might as well have married Lorimer in the first place, without insisting upon those long months of probation. As he had watched the progress of that merry supper in Arlt's honor, Thayer had been distressed about Lorimer and about the scene which must inevitably follow; but his distress had been as nothing in comparison with his disappointment in Beatrix.

In reality, Beatrix had had no responsibility in the matter.

"I don't see any need of our having champagne, Sidney," she had said, on the morning that they had first discussed the detail of the supper.

Lorimer had been in one of his old-time moods. Now he laughed a little.

"What a Puritan you are, Beatrix!" he said, as he bent caressingly over her shoulder to read the completed list of guests.

"Not a Puritan," she urged; "but I would rather not have the champagne, Sidney. It isn't at all necessary; we can get on perfectly well without it."

"And a good deal better with it," he retorted, laughing. "Well, never mind it now, dear girl. But what about a florist?"

And Beatrix, delighted at her easy victory, had allowed herself to be led off into a consideration of the decorations for the table. She could not be expected to foresee that, in giving the final orders for the supper, Lorimer would include a generous allowance of champagne. Neither could she have foreseen that one of the invitations would find its way into the hands of Lloyd Avalons. Confronted suddenly by both the champagne and Lloyd Avalons, Beatrix had faltered only for a moment. Then she had rallied to meet the inevitable crisis so swiftly that no one but Bobby Dane at her elbow had been aware of her momentary weakness. Thayer had been at the other end of the room, and had missed the instant of hesitation. By the time he had discovered the situation, Beatrix had forced herself to meet it as a matter of course. She faltered a second time, however, as she met the questioning glance which Thayer gave her. She had learned to care for his good opinion; she knew that now she was in danger of forfeiting it. Nevertheless, her loyalty to her husband was paramount. Never by a spoken word had she implied to Thayer that Lorimer was falling below her ideals. To-night, hurt as she was by his deception, anxious as she was in regard to the outcome of the episode, nevertheless she remained true to her usual careful reticence. To a woman of Beatrix Lorimer's temper it was easier to bear unjust blame than to demand just pity. And yet, as she recognized that the facts were apparently all against her, she could not help hoping that Thayer would suspend judgment until he had talked with Bobby Dane. Bobby had seen the memoranda for the supper, and had advised her in regard to some of the details. Not only was he the one person besides herself and Lorimer who knew the whole truth; but he could invariably be relied upon to tell the truth in its entirety.

As Lorimer had said, it was a great night for Arlt. His work had scored a complete success, and he had been called twice before the audience to receive in person his applause. Something in the simple overture had caught the fancy of the orchestra, and they had played it with an enthusiasm, had interpreted it with a dainty accuracy to Arlt's own mood which would have won prompt recognition for a work of far less merit. The critics were warm in their praises; but the audience, upon whom a popular success depends far more than upon the professional leaders of opinion, was in a mood to be expressed by no such temperate phrase. As he lingered in the Lorimers' box, watching the young German come forward to the footlights, Thayer was ready to predict a fair measure of lasting popularity to his friend. The audience was most hospitable to him. It now remained for the Lorimers' supper to set upon him the seal of social approval. For Arlt's sake, Thayer devoutly hoped that the supper would be a success. Under other conditions, he might have had his doubts. This was the first time he had seen Lorimer for weeks; but the stories which had drifted to his ears had not been reassuring. In Lorimer's own house, however, there could be no danger. He felt that he could count upon Beatrix to forestall that.

In the weeks since they had met, it seemed to him that Beatrix must have grown more beautiful with each passing day. Beneath the perfect poise of her manner, he could see an increasing gentleness, a sadness which was under absolute control. She was as strong as ever, but less self-reliant. Experience had taught her that she was powerless to fight alone. In her worst battles, she had learned that she must rely upon another; and Thayer, as he watched her, rejoiced that that other was himself. His weeks of separation from her, of enforced forgetfulness, had taught him a lesson which he had been loath to learn. Rather than be outside her world, rather than be upon the same footing as all the other inhabitants of that world, he would gladly endure a strain like that of the past summer, would accept the place where fate had put him, as the one man who could make more tolerable her own life with her husband. It was not a dignified position; yet, for her sake, he believed that he could fill it in a way which would add dignity to the lives of them both. At least, he would do the best that was in him. He took no account of the possibility that, within an hour, he would be balked in his efforts by certain uninfringible laws of hospitality.

"Moreover," Lorimer went on, still in that unwonted high, clear voice; "le's drink to Arlt's mother an' sister, Frau Arlt an' Fräulein Katarina Arlt."

The sudden angry color blazed up in Arlt's cheeks, and he straightened in his chair. Then he caught Thayer's eye, and with an effort he controlled himself. The instant's by-play had caused Thayer to lose the next words of his host; but Lorimer's laugh was ringing out with such infectious mirth that the guests were laughing with him, although with obvious reluctance to show their merriment.

Lorimer babbled on discursively.

"I knew 'em well. They were having har' times to get on, an' Arlt here could n' begin to carry the load. It was killing him, an' so Thayer an' I--"

"Let the rest go, Lorimer," Thayer broke in hastily, for now two appealing faces were looking to him for help. "We know all about it."

Lorimer turned to him with an air of grave rebuke.

"You know, Thayer, for you were there. But the res' do' know. How could they? They were n' there." He paused long enough to empty the glass before him. Then he braced one hand against the edge of the table and raised the other, as if to add emphasis to his words. "I was there, an' you were there, an' Arlt was there. Nobody else was there. If they had been, they'd know 'bout it, to-night. Plucky fellow, Arlt, an' he d'serves his success. If 't had n' been for you an' me, Thayer, Arlt would have gone under, though. No wond' Frau Arlt calls me *Lieb Sohn*. If it had n' been for me, she would n' have had any *sohn* 't all. With me, there's pair of us."

He delivered himself of this long speech with an air of portentous gravity. Then he turned away from Thayer and smiled benignly up the table. Side by side at the farther end, Arlt and Beatrix seemed powerless to take their eyes from his face. Lorimer caught the eye of Beatrix and instantly his face lighted, as he kissed his hand to her.

"Supper's a gran' success, dear girl," he called gayly. "Ought to be, cost 'nough, an' has been no end trouble; but it pays. People will know wha' we think of Arlt now. He's geniush, 'n no mishtake; are n' you, Arlt?"

"Bobby," Sally whispered; "I must go away, I can't bear this for another minute."

Bobby nodded comprehendingly.

"Slip out, the next time he begins on Thayer. I think you can do it, and you oughtn't to stay. I wish the others would go, too."

"They may follow me. I would break it up, if I dared; but--Bobby, I'm afraid."

"So am I," Bobby growled through his shut teeth. "Come back in the morning, Sally. Beatrix may need you. I'd go with you now; but I dare not leave things."

But Lorimer's eye was upon them.

"Wha' now, Sally?" he asked jovially. "Bobby been making a bad pun, that you look so savage?"

Sally hesitated. For one instant, she eyed her host as if he had been a scorpion that had crawled across her path. Then she controlled herself, and her voice took on its customary mocking drawl.

"No; I only feel savage because I know you must have set the clocks ahead. Just see! It is high time we all were going home, and you know I always hate to start."

Lorimer glanced at the clock on the mantel. Then he turned to the man behind his chair.

"Stop tha' clock!" he commanded. "We can' have anybody talk 'bout going home yet. Night's only jus' begun, an' there's quarts more champagne. Beatrix did n' wan' us to have any; but I don' believe in being stingy."

Sally had already risen, and one or two other women, casting furtive, apologetic glances towards Beatrix, were hurriedly following Sally's example. In the slight confusion, it seemed to Thayer that his chance had come, and he took it. Unfortunately, however, for the once he had reckoned without his man. He had kept careful count of the glasses which Lorimer had emptied since he had sat down at the table, and he knew that the danger limit was not far distant. In fact, the danger limit was already passed. Thayer had had no means of taking into account the glasses which Lorimer had slyly emptied, during his short absence from the room before they had gone to the table. The mischief was already done. The slightest shock which could disturb Lorimer's present mood would be sufficient to destroy his whole mental balance past any possibility of restoration. Thayer's error in judgment promptly furnished the shock.

Lorimer had turned again to the butler at the back of his chair.

"Fill thish up," he demanded, as he pointed to his glass.

With a swift gesture, Thayer caught the man's attention, and shook his head. The man hesitated, halting between two masters. The one paid him his wages; the other commanded his entire respect, and it was not easy for him to choose the one whom he should obey.

"Fill thish up, I shay!" Lorimer's voice was thicker, his accent imperious.

Swiftly the old butler glanced at Thayer as if for instructions, and Thayer again shook his head. This time, Lorimer saw the signal. The next instant, his empty glass was flying straight in the direction of Thayer's face.

There was a frightened outcry from the women; but Thayer swerved slightly to one side, and the glass crashed harmlessly against the mantel. There followed the tinkle of the falling pieces, then a stillness so profound that from one end to the other of the long room Lorimer's heavy breathing was distinctly audible. The impending crisis seemed to paralyze the guests. Those who had risen, stood motionless in their places; the others made no effort to rise. They remained there together, silent, passive, tense, with Lorimer facing them all, like a savage beast at bay.

[Illustration: "Beatrix still sat at the disordered table"]

The interval, seemingly so endless, lasted only for a moment. Then, with a beast-like snarl, Lorimer sprang up, overturning his chair, and hurled himself straight upon Thayer. Strong as he was, Thayer tottered before the blow, for the strength of Lorimer just then was far beyond the human. Drink-crazed and brutalized, he had the fierce power of a maddened brute. There was a swift, sharp struggle, broken by strange, inarticulate cries, making the women hide their faces and cram their fingers into their ears to shut out sight and sound. Then the struggle grew still again, and they heard Thayer's steady voice saying,--

"I think he is quiet now. Dane, will you help me to carry him to his room?"

One by one, the terrified guests slank away. There were no good-nights scarcely a whispered word in the dressing-rooms upstairs. At length, they were all gone, and the house was still. The lights from the open windows glared out across the night, and the rooms inside were heavy with the fragrance of roses and the smell of champagne. Upstairs in Lorimer's room, Thayer and Bobby Dane were watching the lethargic sleep which had fallen upon their host, and counting the moments until Arlt could bring the doctor back with him. Downstairs, alone in the abandoned dining-room, Beatrix still sat at the disordered table, with her head bowed forward upon her clasped hands.

CHAPTER EIGHTEEN

"It's a devilish mess, do what you will," Bobby said grimly, the next morning.

"The punishment seems a good deal out of proportion to the cause," Thayer replied briefly.

"Hh!" Bobby grunted. "I think he did well to get off without a genuine case of D. T."

"I was speaking of your cousin, not of Lorimer."

Bobby stared at him in astonishment.

"Really, Thayer, I can't see any cause that was of Beatrix's making," he returned haughtily.

"It was mistaken judgment, to say the least, to have champagne in the house," Thayer answered.

"Beatrix had nothing to do with that," Bobby blazed forth angrily. "It was that brute of a Lorimer, and he deserves all he got, and more, too. I saw the order to the caterer, made out in Beatrix's handwriting, and there wasn't a pint of champagne on it. Lorimer sent in the order afterwards, just as he invited that serpent of a Lloyd Avalons. Beatrix couldn't help herself."

"She could have countermanded the order."

"She didn't know it till the guests were there. I was with her when she discovered it, and she took it like a heroine. She was perfectly helpless. She couldn't make a scene in her own house, and she couldn't reasonably be expected to send her guests home. She knew exactly what was bound to happen, what she couldn't help happening, and she kept her head steady and faced the thing as boldly as she could. I never thought you would be the one to go back on her, Thayer."

Thayer started to speak. Then he squared his jaw, and was silent. After a long interval, he said humbly,--

"I have wronged your cousin, Dane. I am very sorry."

"So am I," Bobby returned flatly. "Beatrix has come to where she needs every friend she owns in the world to stand by her. By to-night, the story of that supper will have spread from the Battery to Poughkeepsie bridge. It will be garbled and twisted into all manner of shapes, and it will come boomeranging back at her from every quarter of the town. When it comes to gossip, we find Manhattan Island is a mighty small place; but I suppose Australia is just as bad."

Thayer interrupted his meditations ruthlessly.

"How is Lorimer, this morning? You've been to the house, I suppose."

"Yes, I've just come from there. Lorimer is convalescent, which means he is a blamed sight better than he deserves to be. I didn't care to see him; but they assured me he was sitting up and regaling himself on raw oysters and chicken broth. He is probably an edifying spectacle by this time, a mush of maudlin penitence. I've seen him before this in his next-morning mood. Put not your trust in a moral jellyfish!" And Bobby, his fists in his pockets, stamped up and down the room to ease his resentment. "The next move is to be a radical one," he continued, after a pause. "They are going into the Adirondacks."

Thayer looked up sharply.

"They? Who?"

"Beatrix and Lorimer."

"What for?"

"Safety; taking to the woods, and all that."

"What do you mean, Dane?" Thayer asked sternly. "This is no time for joking. Do speak out."

"I beg your pardon, Thayer. The fact is, I am utterly reckless, this morning, and I don't know nor care what I am saying. If you loved Beatrix as I do--"

"Yes," Thayer returned quietly. "I understand."

"No; you don't. You can't. We've been such chums. What hurts her, hurts me; and, to my dying day, I shall never forget her as we found her in the dining-room, last night. She knew then it was all over." Bobby's voice broke upon the last words; then he pulled himself up sharply. "This morning, we had a council of war, Mrs. Dane and Beatrix and the doctor and I. The doctor says that Beatrix isn't well, and that another such scene would kill her, or worse. I was for shutting Lorimer up in an inebriate asylum; but Beatrix opposed the idea. She was so excited about it that the doctor finally took sides with her, and said that she and Lorimer would better not be separated, at least, not until something else comes up. Do you grasp the pleasant state of things? Lorimer is to be left with her till something does come up; when the something does come, it may kill her. That's what they call an alternative, I suppose."

"But the Adirondacks?" Thayer reminded him. It was unlike Bobby Dane to go off like this into conversational blind alleys. Thayer, as he listened and looked at his friend's haggard face, realized suddenly that Bobby was far less superficial than was generally supposed.

"The doctor ordered them both out of town. It is the only way to keep Lorimer out of mischief, get him into the wilderness to live on venison and bromides. We chose the Adirondacks because it was near and safe, and because we could tell people that Beatrix needed the air. Of course, they'll know we are lying; but we may as well lie valiantly and plausibly, while we are about it."

"When do they go?"

"Monday."

"Who goes?"

"They hire a cottage, and take enough servants to run it. Then there will be a man for Lorimer. The doctor insisted upon that."

"Who else?"

"Beatrix and Lorimer."

"And Mrs. Dane?"

"No; no one else."

"You don't mean that Mrs. Lorimer is going up into that wilderness alone?"

"Alone with her liege lord," Bobby said bitterly.

"But she mustn't. It's not safe."

"Who can go? Mrs. Dane is not strong; she would only be an extra care for Beatrix."

"Mr. Dane, then."

"He's no use. I would go, myself; but I can't well get off. Besides, Lorimer hates me, and my being there would only make it harder for Beatrix. Do you really think she ought to have someone?" Bobby's voice was anxious.

"For nine days, no; for the tenth, yes," Thayer said decidedly. "We both know that, some time or other, Lorimer is bound to go on another spree. No; there's no use in being too hard on him. The time has passed, if it ever existed, when he was as responsible as you would be, or I. It's in his blood, and he has lost all his nerve to fight it out. But, when that spree comes, if it comes while they are up there, Mrs. Lorimer must have someone to stand back of her. Who is there?"

Bobby shook his head.

"I don't know," he confessed. "I would go, if I could; but I can't."

There was a long silence between the two men. Thayer, sitting at his desk, was absently measuring his blotting pad with a letter, so many envelopes' length this way, so many that. The letter was from the impresario, reminding him that his decision was due, that night, and urging him to accept the offer. At length, Thayer turned around away from the desk, and faced Bobby.

"Is there a hotel near there?" he asked.

"Half a mile away."

"Open at this season?"

"Yes, there are always cranks and consumptives, you know."

Thayer faced back again and measured the blotter anew. Then he tossed the letter aside and, rising, walked across to the mantel.

"I think I'll go up there for a little while," he said briefly.

"Thayer! You can't."

"Why not?"

"Because you mustn't. It's impossible."

Thayer mistook his meaning.

"I can't see the impossibility, Dane. Lorimer was--is my friend. I knew him long before I ever heard of Mrs. Lorimer. I was their guest at Monomoy for a month, last summer, too. We both of us know that I can hold Lorimer, when nobody else can. I don't pretend to understand it, myself; but the fact remains. All in all, I think I am the best possible person to go."

His voice was quiet, yet its every accent was final and uncompromising. Before its dignity, Bobby felt like a rebuked child. He hastened to justify himself.

"I wasn't thinking of that at all, Thayer. The idea would have been an insult both to you and to Beatrix. I know that Beatrix feels she can rely on you to manage Lorimer; but nevertheless it is absolutely out of the question for you to go."

"Why?"

"Your engagements for the winter."

"I have made no engagements yet."

"Is that a fact?"

"As a general rule, I tell the truth," Thayer answered dryly.

"Well, you are sure to make some."

"Perhaps. When I do, it will be time enough for me to keep them."

"But your reputation!" Bobby urged.

"What of it?"

"How is it going to stand your burying yourself in the wilderness, just when you have the city at your feet?"

"It will have to stand it. It will, if it is worth anything at all."

"Thayer, you sha'n't!" Bobby protested. "It's Quixotic and idiotic. You sha'n't spoil your own good life for the sake of Lorimer's bad one. He isn't worth it."

Thayer straightened his shoulders and threw back his head.

"What about Mrs. Lorimer?" he asked steadily.

The clock marked the passing seconds until hundreds of them had gone away, never to return. Then Bobby crossed the room and laid his hand on Thayer's shoulder.

"Thayer," he said slowly; "you are a fool, an utterly asinine fool; but I can't help wishing that there were a few more fools in the world just like you."

And in that instant, it flashed into Bobby Dane's mind that, ever since he had first come to know Cotton Mather Thayer, he had been expecting and awaiting just such a scene.

Late that same afternoon, Miss Gannion's card was brought to Beatrix. All that day, she had denied herself to callers; not even Sally Van Osdel had been admitted. Ten minutes before Miss Gannion came, Beatrix would have said that she too must be sent away; but, as she read the name on the card, she felt a sudden impulsive longing to see her old-time friend.

Miss Gannion wasted no words on conventional greeting.

"You dear child!" she said quietly. "I know a little about what has happened; but it is all I need to know. Talk about it or not, just as you choose."

Urged or repressed, Beatrix would have held herself steady, reticent. All day long, she had kept herself quiet, going through her usual domestic routine, answering notes of invitation and then methodically sorting out the clothing she would need during her absence from town. She had refused her mother's help and she had sent away her maid; it was a relief to her to keep busy. Left to herself and idle, the future easily could have occupied her whole attention; but as yet she was not strong enough to face it. Strange to say, there had been no benumbing effect of her sorrow. From the first hour, she had been able to grasp with dreary clearness all its details, all its effect upon the present and upon the future which now to her was freighted with a double burden of anxiety and alarm.

All day long until late afternoon, she had forced this quiet upon herself; but it could not go on indefinitely. Already the tug and wrench upon her nerves was slackening, and Miss Gannion's words brought the swift revulsion. The older woman shrank before the storm of passionate sorrow. Then she braced herself to bear it, for she realized that it was the flood which must inevitably follow the breaking down of the dykes that for months had pent in the seas of a daily and hourly agony such as a weaker soul than that of Beatrix could never know.

It was long before Beatrix dared trust her voice to speak, and then Miss Gannion was startled at the utter dreariness of her tone.

"It has all been a horrible mistake," she said slowly. "I thought I was stronger. I did believe that I could hold him, Miss Gannion. I didn't rush into it carelessly, as most girls do. I knew all the danger. I thought about it, and measured it against my strength and against the strength of his love. I truly thought I could hold him."

"I know, dear," Miss Gannion said gently. "I thought so, too."

"But I couldn't. I did try, try my best. But it was no use. And yet, he did love me, just as I did love him."

"Did love?" Miss Gannion questioned, for Beatrix had paused, as if challenging her.

"Yes, did love. My love is dead, Miss Gannion."

"But it may come back."

"Never. It never can. He has killed it utterly. I am sorry. I don't know why I am telling you, for no one else must know it, not even Sidney himself. He doesn't suspect it at all now, and I mean that he never shall. If I made the mistake in the first place, I ought to be the one to suffer for it, not he."

"But he loves you now," Miss Gannion said unsteadily.

"To-day. Yesterday, he forgot me entirely; to-day, he cares for me just as he always has done, no more, no less. I wish I could care for him; but I can't. I feel perfectly cold, as if nothing more could ever warm me."

"But, in time--after you have forgotten last night--"

Beatrix shook her head.

"My love for Sidney did not die, last night. It was too strong, too much alive, to be killed by the facts of one single night. No; it had been ailing for months; but it finally died, six weeks ago, and nothing now can ever make it live again. Miss Gannion, I have been very selfish."

"I don't think so, Beatrix."

But Beatrix gently drew herself out of Miss Gannion's arms, rose and stood looking down at her friend. In that moment, confronted by Beatrix's sad, calm face and luminous eyes, the little gray-haired woman suddenly realized that, notwithstanding the difference in their years, Beatrix was looking into mysteries which were far beyond her ken.

"Yes, I was selfish," Beatrix went on steadily. "I loved Sidney; I was happy in his love, and I believed that, through both our loves, I could be strong enough to save him from himself. I knew it was a risk, a terrible risk, but I took it for granted that the risk would come only on myself, and, for both our sakes, I was willing to assume it. I was nothing but a child, for all I felt so wise, and I stopped there, without looking ahead. I was wrong, woefully, sinfully wrong. I was selfish, for I thought of nothing beyond myself. Now that it is too late, I am beginning to realize what it all may mean to the next generation."

CHAPTER NINETEEN

"O the long and dreary Winter! O the cold and cruel Winter!"

Thayer's voice was wonderfully rich and mellow, as he stood at the window softly singing over to himself that haunting, tragic Famine Theme from *The Death of Minnehaha*. Fresh from its weeks of resting, low, yet suggesting an immeasurable reserve power, it had all its old throbbing magnetism; but a new quality had been added to it. It had always had moments of passionate appeal; now it had gained a sadness, a depth of melancholy which in the past it had been powerless to express. A year before, Thayer could strike the tragic note, never the pathetic.

Nevertheless, the pathos was apparently merely a matter of the vocal cords. The tall, alert, well-groomed man who stood at the snow-veiled window in no way suggested being a candidate for sympathy. His eyes were clear, his brows unfurrowed. Moreover, one could never dream of condoling with the owner of such a voice. Taken quite by itself, its possession would outweigh an almost infinite number of human woes.

"Ever thicker, thicker, thicker Froze the ice on lake and river, Ever deeper, deeper, deeper Fell the snow--"

Hiawatha's wigwam might well have been just beyond the spruce thicket, Thayer reflected. The description was too accurate to be artistic; it amounted to mere photography. As far as his own eyes could see, the earth lay buried in a deep, soft blanket of snow, and the air above was misty with flakes which neither fell nor scurried before the wind, but hung apparently motionless in the still, cold air. All through the preceding night, however, the wind had blown fiercely. The snow lay heaped in heavy, irregular drifts across the open plain; but under the trees it was rolled up into soft waves whose tops curled over as daintily as the waves had curled over on the moonlit beach of Monomoy. The lake was frozen over and snow-covered; but the creek that came rushing down to meet it was too swift to be overtaken by the frost, and it showed, an inky-dark, sinuous line of open water, winding away and away among the trees, now losing itself in a thicket of alders, now drawing a straight black mark across an open stretch of meadow where the frost-flowers on its banks offered a delicate substitute for their summer kin.

Half a mile away to the south, the mountain rose abruptly, its face of sheer rock making a dark scar on the winter landscape, a scar crossed with long white bands and bars of ice which, glacier-wise, were creeping over the edge of the cliff as if seeking to veil its sinister face. Against the base of the mountain, close to the inky creek, another patch of darkness stood out in bold relief. This patch was the Lorimers' cottage.

In spite of the haunting melancholy of his song, Thayer looked out at the cottage and at the storm with a feeling of supreme content. Lorimer hated storms with a catlike fervor; it was an old-time peculiarity of his, dating from their student days in Göttingen. There was no likelihood of his leaving the cottage, that day; and, inside the cottage with his man to look out for him, Thayer felt that he was beyond the possibility of danger. It was seven weeks since they had buried themselves in that wilderness, seven weeks that Thayer had voluntarily kept himself under the daily and hourly strain of constant intimate association with the woman he loved, of knowing that she gained strength and courage from her reliance upon him, and of forcing himself to treat her with an offhand good-fellowship which defied analysis for the mere reason that it challenged none.

A weaker man than Thayer would have yielded to the strain, or else have grown fretful under its chafing. Thayer did neither. He felt the chafing, galling burden which he bore; but he kept the scars out of sight of others, and moreover, he conscientiously refrained from looking at them, himself. Self-pity is the surest, yet the most insidious foe to self-poise. When the original Cotton Mather Thayer had stuck a splinter of wood into the palm of his hand, he had pulled out the splinter with his teeth and then, punching his hand into his pocket, he had continued his discussion of the latest election to the General Court. His namesake was proving himself true to the traditions of his blood.

Twice only had Thayer sought outlet for his mood. Twice the almost deserted hotel had vibrated with such singing as it was destined never to have heard, before or since. The piano was passable and, shut up alone in the barren parlor, Thayer had sung to the empty chairs as he had never yet sung to any crowded audience. Out in the halls, the people of the house gathered in listening, whispering groups; but Thayer never heeded them. It is not certain that, heeding, he would have cared. Relief he must have at any cost, and this was the one means at his command. His own voice, laden with passionate sadness, came echoing back to him from the unresponsive walls, and in time the echo checked his outcry. It taught him anew the lesson which already he had conned again and again, the lesson that his bitterest plaint fell on no one else's ears with half the compelling fervor with which it reached his own, that his cry for help came beaten back to the one person who could help him, that was--himself. But at least, there was some relief in having made his cry.

He had never allowed himself to regret his answer to the impresario. Day by day, he realized more and more keenly that his presence there was imperative. Beatrix seemed to him far from well. Her nerves had been less steady since the shock of that last supper in New York; she was totally unable to adjust herself to Lorimer's swift alternations of mood, his hours of demonstrative affection, his times of black depression and irritability. Thayer saw that she did her best, that she bravely sought to play a loyal part in the work of reformation. The failure was in no sense that of will, but of mere nervous strength. But there were hours and hours when Thayer stood between them, trying by his sympathy for Lorimer to atone for Beatrix's coldness, trying by his chivalry to Beatrix to make amends for the fractiousness of Lorimer.

There were hours when he mourned acutely for his work. They invariably followed upon the heels of a letter from Arlt and they invariably ended in his going to the cottage and dragging Lorimer out for a tramp in the stinging air. The doctor had ordered much exercise, and Lorimer, who refused to go beyond his door in the society of his man, made long expeditions at Thayer's side, returning weary of body, but of placid mood and healthy appetite, to spend a short evening and a long and restful night.

The day before, they had been out since early morning. The deep-packed snow had lain, hard and solid and tempting, and the sun glittered coldly back into the windless air. Lorimer had been in high spirits. One of his old gay, infectious moods was upon him, and, for the passing hour, Thayer let himself yield to it until he forgot Beatrix, forgot the tragedy which overhung them all, forgot even the number of miles they had come. At noon, they had found a wood-choppers' camp and, sitting around the blazing fire, they had mingled their daintily-packed lunch with the cruder fare of their temporary hosts. Lorimer had been the life of the party, and the good-bys had been spoken with real regret. At the top of the hill above the camp, Lorimer had turned back again to wave his cap in boyish farewell. Then the episode had ended, ended more completely than Thayer as yet could realize.

Lorimer's mood changed on the way home. He grumbled about the softening snow, about the gathering dusk, about the length of the road. His exasperation reached its height when, ignoring Thayer's advice in regard to the path, he struck out across an open snowfield, only to go crashing down through its insecure foundation of baby spruces whose lusty little branches bore up the snow like myriad arms. When Lorimer emerged from the shallow caverns beneath, his temper was of the blackest, and, all the rest of the way home, he had stalked along in gloomy silence, ten feet in the rear of his companion's heels.

Thayer had judged that it would be well to invite himself to stay to dinner at the cottage. Lorimer had been in one of his worst moods, and even Thayer had found it wellnigh impossible to keep the talk brisk and amicable. He had remained until he had seen that Lorimer was at last yielding to the inevitable drowsiness of his long day in the open air; then he had started back to the hotel. Once outside the cottage, however, he had squared his shoulders and drawn a deep breath of relief. He needed mental ozone; but even physical ozone was better than mental nitrous oxide.

And now he was standing at the snow-veiled window, looking across at the cottage while he hummed to himself the recurring, haunting Famine Theme,--

"O the famine and the fever! O the wasting of the famine! O the blasting of the fever!"

He had no notion of the truth of his words. Had he done so, the cottage, not the hotel, would have held him, that day, and the tragedy, so long averted, might have been warded off a little longer. But fate willed otherwise. To Thayer's mind, Lorimer, storm-bound and weary from his tramp of the day before, would spend the day, drowsing, novel in hand, before the open fire. Thayer, in his own absolute integrity, could never imagine the truth: that Lorimer's trusty attendant had at last yielded to the temptation of the oft-repeated bribe and had given into Lorimer's hands the bottle from which he was used to measure out, medicine-wise, the daily lessening allowance of brandy. He could not know how often, all that day, Beatrix went to the window and looked out across the storm in the hope of seeing him come striding to her through the snow. Had it been possible, she would have sent for him; but it was a day when women are safest inside a house, and she dared not remove either Lorimer's man or the old butler from their close guard over her husband. She had been utterly opposed to bringing the faithful old butler with them; but now she was glad that she had yielded to his begging. He had been with her father since her childhood, and had insisted upon following "Miss Beatrix" into her new home. Without him now, she would have been absolutely, hopelessly alone.

Thayer spent a quiet, contented day. For the time being, he had dismissed Lorimer from his mind, and he gave himself up to the luxury of taking thought for no one but himself. The sensation was very luxurious from its very novelty. He wrote a long letter to Arlt, responded to a dozen notes of invitation which had pursued him from the city, loitered about the office and ended the day with a novel which had reached him when the mail came in, that noon. It was still early when he went to bed. As he drew the shades, from sheer force of habit he glanced across at the cottage. Its lights were burning brightly, their quiet steadiness giving no hint of the hideous carnival within.

No healthy man can go to bed, two hours before his usual time, and expect to sleep peacefully till dawn. At four o'clock, Thayer waked suddenly, with the firm belief that his slumber must have reached quite around the clock. He struck a match and looked at his watch.

Restlessly he rose and began to walk up and down the room. The storm had increased during the night. He could hear the snow sifting against the windows and, far off at a distant corner of the house, a loosened blind was beating to and fro in the wind. The sound echoed drearily through the almost deserted barracks, and added infinitely to the loneliness of the wilderness, and of the night, and of the storm.

Thayer paused at the window, raised the shade and peered out into the night. At first, he could see only the darkness, no longer black, but gray with the swirling snow. The ceaseless, pitiless fall of the flakes fascinated him, and he stood long, watching them take shape in the distance, come whirling against the glass and slide aimlessly down the pane, as so many had fallen before them. Then, as the storm lost something of its fury, he glanced up and out across the night. The next instant, his face was pressed against the pane, while his clasped fingers shielded his eyes from the light within the room. In the Lorimers' cottage, half a mile away, the lights were still burning. On such a night and at such an hour, those lights meant trouble: illness, or perhaps something infinitely worse.

He had stood at the window longer than he had realized, and the clock in the office struck five as Thayer, fully dressed, stepped out into the hall. With the waning of the night, the storm was increasing again and, strong man as he was, Thayer faltered as he opened the door and went out into the darkness.

Four times he tried to beat his way against the wind, to force a path through the wet, heavy drifts. Four times, buffeted and almost spent, he was driven back to the shelter of the veranda. The office clock struck six, as he went inside the house to find a shivering servant sweeping out the office.

"Get me some snowshoes," he ordered briefly. "The lights have burned all night in Mr. Lorimer's cottage; I am afraid they may be ill and in need of help. I thought I could get to them; but in this storm it is impossible, unless I can have some shoes."

By some trick of the brain, anxious and impatient as he was, the Famine Theme recurred to his mind, and the servant, coming back with the shoes, found him singing it softly to himself. The words died away into inarticulate humming, as Thayer bent over to fasten the straps. Then, buttoning his coat closely and pulling his cap down over his eyes, Thayer opened the door for the second time and went striding away across the gray, tempestuous darkness which had shut down again impenetrably between himself and those steady, ominous lights.

CHAPTER TWENTY

"It has all been a hideous mistake!"

Abruptly, defiantly Beatrix threw out the words at Thayer, as he entered. Then her head dropped on her arms which rested on the table before her.

Breathless from his struggle with the storm and astounded at her greeting, Thayer halted just across the threshold and looked at her in silence. The silence grew irksome to her. She changed the form of her words.

"I couldn't help it. I have tried." The defiance in her voice suddenly gave place to desperation. She pushed back her chair, rose and crossed the room to the fire. There she turned and stood facing Thayer, her head erect, her cheeks scarlet, her hands, palms downward, tightly clasped. "I have tried my best and failed. It is a total, absolute failure," she went on fiercely. "I know it, and you know it, too. You have watched it coming on, growing and overpowering me. We may as well admit it; I made a mistake when I married Sidney Lorimer."

Thayer met her eyes steadily, rallying all his forces to face her in this new mood. This sudden change in her baffled his powers of comprehension. Weakened and torn and shaken by her endless hours alone in the whistling, roaring storm, listening moment by moment to the hideous noises of delirium coming from the next room, the level nerves of Beatrix had at last given way completely. The noises had stopped now, and an ominous stillness lay over the room; but in Beatrix's ears they still were ringing, beating a terrible accompaniment to the crowding measures of her thoughts. Hour after hour as she had sat alone, her fingers in her ears, her eyes fixed on the snow-draped landscape outside the window, her mind had worked ceaselessly, arbitrarily. For the time being, she had felt herself unable to control the direction of her thoughts, and the direction had been fraught with danger.

She went back to her first meeting with Lorimer. She went over each detail of their friendship and of their married life. She tried in vain to connect the genial, fascinating man she had first known with the man whose ravings found their way under her fingers pressed against her ears. She recalled his old-time devotion and chivalry; she contrasted it with his moodiness and the brutal petulance which of late had marked his manner to her. At no one point had there been a sudden change in him. The transition had been slow, insidious. At last she had wakened to it in all its bald reality.

Now and then she rose and went to the window in the hope of seeing Thayer's familiar figure coming towards her through the storm. Each time she did so, her thoughts lingered a little upon him, upon his power to hold Lorimer, upon his constant thoughtfulness for her. Each time she thought of him, her mind rested there longer, until she found herself going over their acquaintance much as, a few hours earlier, she had gone over her life with Lorimer. Then, all at once, she dropped her head on the table with a little moan. Her will was powerless longer to blind her to the truth. Her loyalty to Lorimer, her traditions, her training had made her fight for months, a fight no less bitter because it was subconscious. Now her fighting strength was gone. The truth had asserted itself at the instant when her nervous force was at its weakest. It had asserted itself, and it had mastered her.

She was still in the passive stage of defeat, when Thayer entered the room, hours later. Struggling to her through the storm, he had been urged on by a fierce passion of anxiety for the woman he loved. A strange fire had flashed up within him, and, had he found Beatrix in her usual mood, he might have lost his power to quench it. Met by a passion equal to his own, he instinctively pulled himself together. Two such storms must inevitably have landed them upon hidden rocks and wrecked them pitilessly and in mid-career. He realized the danger. It took all his manhood to face it; but two lives were trembling in the balance, with nothing but his own past character and half of his inherited tendencies to act as a fulcrum.

"I am afraid I don't quite understand you," he said.

"Then what are you doing here?" she returned sharply.

Thayer faltered. Then,--

"I thought perhaps you might be in need of help," he said quietly.

Her lip curled, and her slender wrists grew tense with the strain upon them.

"For what? John and Patrick can take care of my husband. Mr. Lorimer is--very ill; but we are quite capable of taking care of him. Why should I need help?" She watched him in silent hostility. Then, as she saw the sudden drawing of his lips, her mood changed. This was her friend, the only friend who was near her and loyal to her. She must not hurt him with her bitterness, lest he too should fail her, just as Lorimer already had done. For months, she had unconsciously depended upon his loyalty. Now she sought it consciously. "What is the use of keeping up the pretence any longer?" she went on drearily. "You have been with us day after day; you know how things are going; you know how my husband has--that he has not always been himself." Even in her desperation, she still chose her words guardedly. "Do you think I ever could have held him?"

Slowly Thayer shook his head.

"No," he said in a low voice. "No; you never could have held him. It was impossible."

"Then why didn't you warn me?" she burst out hotly.

He looked her straight in the eye.

"How could I?"

Her face flushed with the sudden understanding. Then the old dreary note came back into her voice.

"And you have known from the first that it was all a mistake?"

"Yes."

"And you have let me suffer for it?"

"You are not the only one," he said, almost involuntarily.

Their eyes met, held each other, then dropped apart. Thayer drew a long, slow breath.

"Mrs. Lorimer--Beatrix--"

She checked him with a gesture.

"Wait! You don't know it all, you can't know. You never knew Sidney Lorimer as I did, for my Sidney Lorimer never really existed. I idealized him, half-deified him. The Sidney Lorimer to whom I gave my love, my very life, was one man; the Sidney Lorimer I married was quite another. A woman can't love two men totally unlike each other, and yet I am bound to him, bound down to the day of my death, or of his. We both come of a long-lived race, and this must go on for years. I have tried to prevent it, this gradual change in him; but it was impossible. Then I tried not to see it; but I had to see it. It insisted on itself and on being seen. I have been watching it, dreading the time when I must admit it in so many words. I have tried to be loyal to him, God knows!" She spoke rapidly. Then she checked herself, and the dreary note came again. "But what is done, is done. I loved one man; I am married to another. Nothing now can bring back to me the man I used to know, the man I used to imagine him. Then what will the future amount to? We shall go on together to the end, two prisoners bound by a chain which only holds us the tighter and galls us the more, the looser it grows between us. One doesn't mind the dying; it's the limitless, unchanging years ahead, the black, blank years that frighten me. How can I escape them?"

In presence of a woman's passionate pain, every man must stand back, baffled and powerless to help. Thayer had supposed he understood Beatrix Lorimer as no other man had ever understood her. To his eyes, her character seemed crystal clear; yet now, in her supreme crisis, the crystal grew cloudy before his eyes. For long hours, she had gone into the deep places of her life, had stirred up from its very source the spring of her being, and the superficial clearness had grown turgid with the dregs that had lain undisturbed and unsuspected there. Hatred and black despair were boiling in the heart which Thayer had thought so calm and cool, so peaceful in its dainty whiteness. Before it, he stood silent. Was this the true Beatrix Lorimer? The woman he had fancied her was a spotless white lily. The heart of this one was banded with bars of flame and gold. The other grew colorless and cold by comparison, and his hands twitched to pluck this fiery, vivid thing before him and carry it away out of reach of Lorimer's sodden, defiling touch. What had Sidney Lorimer, drunkard, profligate that he was, to do with this high-bred, high-spirited, heart-broken woman? Why not rather he, Cotton Mather Thayer--He thrust his hands into his pockets and lowered his eyes to hide the light burning in them.

It seemed to him hours since he had entered the house. In reality, the time was short. As he had crossed the threshold, Beatrix had raised her head and looked at him dully. Then her reaction had come. Like the ebb and flow of the waves, excitement had followed apathy; and, as she had met his eyes, the wave had risen again and swept her away upon its tossing crest. Thayer was here at last. He never forgot her, never forsook her. He had come to her in this moment of her bitterest need, even as he had come to her many a time in the past. With him, there could be no need for explanation or preface. Straight from the heart of her reverie, Beatrix Lorimer had cast her words at him,--

"It has all been a hideous mistake!"

And now she was following them up with the question which, in Thayer's ears, sounded the dominant note of the temptation that had been pursuing him during all those months of rigid self-restraint,--

"The black, blank years, how can I escape them?"

For the second time in his life, Thayer grew dizzy with the tingle of his nerves answering to the shock to his brain. The blood was pounding across his temples, and his ears rang loudly. Then he lifted his eyes deliberately and looked Beatrix full in the face. For an instant, he held her eyes; then she drew away from him. This was not the quiet, self-contained man upon whom she had leaned for months. This man's eyes were glowing, his lips quivering, his hands outstretched to meet her own. No need to tell her what flame had kindled him into such fierce and burning life. Their eyes met. She drew away; but her glance never wavered. Without a spoken word, they had come to the pitiless, naked truth. Wish had answered to wish, and henceforth there could be no concealments between them. She took a step forward, and for a moment her fingers rested in the hot hollow of his hand.

It was only for a moment. However, for Thayer that moment had sufficed to review a lifetime, to dwell in detail, even, upon the events of the last fourteen months. In the past, he had done his best to bear himself as an honest man and a gentleman; and, seen in the light of that past, the future turned to ashes before him. At best, it was void of honor; at worst, it was unthinkable. It had not been easy for him to swim against the tide, to strive, at the expense of his own plans, to rescue Lorimer from drunkenness and shame. At least, now that for so long a time he had succeeded in keeping his head above water, he would not wilfully cast himself upon the first jagged rock in his course. He would not save Lorimer's honor for the sake of Lorimer's wife, and then deliberately seek to bring dishonor and shame upon the wife herself. He veiled his eyes and let his palm drop out from under the pressure of the cold little fingers.

"It's not necessarily a question of years," he said, after a silence in which it seemed to him that she must be able to count his heart-throbs. "Dane told me what the doctor said. He hopes this place will work a complete cure, and it may not be long before your husband pulls himself together again."

He had turned a little away from her; but he knew she was still looking at him. He could feel the pathetic appeal in her eyes, yet he never wavered. However brutal he might seem to her now, he knew that the hour would come when she would be grateful to him.

With an effort, she steadied herself.

"I am afraid it is impossible. He has gone too far; the pull now is all downward."

"What about your hold on him?" Thayer asked quietly.

Beatrix started, as if he had laid a clumsy thumb on an exposed nerve.

"My hold!" she said, with a sudden fierceness. "Do you think that there is no limit to the help which I must give him?" Then her voice dropped. "No; I have let go. It is no use. I have done all I can, and now I can only wait till the play is over and the curtain drops. Perhaps it may not be so very long, after all. It spoils any tragedy, if the last acts drag."

He had been fired by her passion; but he had resisted it. Now her despair unmanned him. It was only the old, old situation: the guiltless one must suffer for the guilty. The fact in general terms he accepted as a necessary evil; the particular instance was unbearable. Once more, and for the last time, the balance wavered; then slowly, steadily it dipped into position. The tragedy would be no less a tragedy, because a new hero took the stage for the final acts. He tried to find words to say; but they refused to come at his bidding. He could only stand mute and look down at her, as she sat in her old place by the table, with her head buried in her arms.

The seconds passed and lengthened into minutes. Little by little, the cold, gray light of the snowy morning was creeping into the room, dimming the lamplight to pale yellow streaks and filling the place with a chill, forbidding gloom. The stillness was so absolute that Thayer could hear his watch ticking in his pocket, could hear the beating of his own heart. Neither one of them moved, or spoke. In the next room, there was a faint sound; but they never heeded it. Beatrix's face was hidden in her arms; Thayer's eyes, turned now to the window, were fixed upon the pitiless storm outside, while mechanically he sought to adjust the regular ticking of his watch to the broken rhythm of the Famine Theme which once more was haunting his brain.

Neither one of them faced the open door; neither one of them saw the crawling, slinking figure, the pale, fear-stricken face, and the staring eyes which appeared in the doorway, clung there for a moment and then vanished again as noiselessly as they had come. Neither of them, had they seen, could have imagined the fearful interpretation which the delirium-stricken brain had put upon the silent scene.

The stir in the next room came again. Then it increased until the cottage echoed with the tumult of struggle and of inarticulate crying. Above it all, Lorimer's maddened voice rang out in piteous terror,--

"Let me go! I saw him! It's Thayer, and he will kill Beatrix! She is afraid of him, and she is begging for mercy! He is killing my wife, my Beatrix! Let me go! Beatrix! Beatrix! Dear girl, I'm coming!"

Beatrix sprang to her feet, as Thayer rushed to the inner room where the words had ended in a fury of inarticulate shrieks. There was the sound of a heavy struggle, when it seemed to her that the cottage rocked with the rocking, writhing bodies of the men just beyond her sight. She dared not face the scene in all its horror. She stood, erect and alone, in the middle of the floor, while the struggle slowly died away and the shrieks sank to the piteous low whimpering of an animal in pain. Then all was still.

Weak by inheritance, weaker still by dissipation, Lorimer's heart had yielded to the shock of his imaginary fear; but the last coherent thought of his distracted brain had been that of protecting love for Beatrix.

In the gray, cold light, through the silent cottage, the old butler came to Beatrix's side and gently touched her arm.

"It is over, Miss Beatrix," he said gravely; "and may the good God be pitiful to us all!"

CHAPTER TWENTY-ONE

It was mid-afternoon when Thayer once more entered the hotel. The proprietor met him at the door.

"This message was just telephoned in, Mr. Thayer. The boy is getting ready to carry it to the cottage."

Thayer tore open the envelope indifferently. Exhausted by the struggle and the shock through which he had been passing, for the time being he felt little interest in any word which could come to him from the outside world. His entire life seemed to him limited to one short hour in one small room, apart from the world and its concerns. That brief episode was too recent and too personal to allow him at once to cast off its impression. In his present mood, it appeared to be the focal point of his entire life, the arena upon which the two warring strains in his blood had met to fight to a finish. The fight had been sharp and fierce; already he was beginning to rejoice that the Puritan had conquered the Slav. Beyond that point, as yet, he was powerless to go. Later, his rejoicing would be increased by the knowledge that in his own words and deeds he had never swerved from a certain loyalty towards Lorimer.

"Mr. Lorimer is--" the proprietor was beginning vaguely.

Thayer's nod was more curt than he realized.

"Mr. Lorimer is dead."

"You don't mean it! When?" The man was visibly startled.

"This morning, between seven and eight o'clock."

"It must have been very sudden?" The accent was plainly interrogative.

"Yes, at the last. He had been quite ill for twenty-four hours. He was overtired with his walk of the day before, and then ate something that disagreed with him. He suffered terribly, and, at the last, heart failure developed." Thayer ended his fable with a deep breath of relief.

"But they had no doctor," the man objected.

Thayer raised his eyes and looked at him steadily for an instant.

"No," he said quietly. "Mr. Lorimer has had a number of such attacks, and Mrs. Lorimer had all the proper remedies. Until within a few moments of the end, there was no indication that this attack was any more serious than the others had been, and there had never before been any tendency to heart failure." He paused for a moment, deliberately challenging another question. Then he added, "If your telephone is not in use, I must send word to Mrs. Lorimer's friends." And he walked away to the telephone closet in the corner of the office.

He called up three numbers in New York. The first one was Mr. Dane's office, and to him Thayer announced the bare fact of Lorimer's death and of Beatrix's need for her parents. His talk with Bobby Dane was longer, and at intervals it became interjectional in its terseness. To Bobby, Thayer went over the story in all its detail, yet in such guarded phrases that no one else, listening, could have gained an inkling of the true cause of Lorimer's death. After the first shock was over, Thayer and Beatrix had discussed the matter fully and in all its bearings. The attendant had his own reasons for wishing to keep the secret, and the butler could be relied upon implicitly. Accordingly, they had decided that there was no need of acquainting the world with the true version of the case, and they had agreed that Bobby should be the one person to be put in possession of all the facts. He was just; he had no sentimental ideals to be dispelled in regard to Lorimer, and he was utterly trustworthy.

Thayer's third message was the shortest of all.

"Not in? Very well. I am Mr. Thayer. Tell him that I will be in his office at ten o'clock on Saturday morning."

It was then late on Thursday afternoon. Thayer had calculated that the Danes would come in, the next day, and that the sleigh which brought them in would also carry him out in season for the night train to New York. There was another illness in the opera company. *Faust* was to be sung on the following Wednesday night, and Thayer, in sending that last message, had given his tacit consent to singing the part of *Valentine*. Even in the midst of his trouble, he smiled grimly to himself, as he thought back to that far-off night in Berlin when the chord which closes *Valentine's* cavatina also closed his long indecision and left him sitting with his face definitely turned towards the artist's life. It had seemed to him then that the decision was threatening to undermine his Puritanism; nevertheless, he had temporized with that Puritanism. In resolving to become an artist, in so far as the possibility of art lay in his keeping, he had likewise resolved to hold himself a man, virile and of steady nerve. To his young enthusiasm, the two ideals had not seemed incompatible. To his maturer judgment, they had appeared in no sense to be at war, yet together they had been by no means easy of attainment. All in all, he had preferred to leave to the recording angel the balancing of his psychological accounts. He had lacked the time and the perspective to do it for himself. But, meanwhile, he believed he recognized the hand of fate in this second summons to sing the part of *Valentine*. Fate and his old *maestro* both had declared themselves for opera. Their united will should be done.

That evening was the longest he had ever spent, so long that in reality it lasted until the gray dawn. The eastern sky was tinging itself with yellow when he roused himself from the reverie which had held him since he had left the dinner table. Rising to his feet, he drew himself to the full of his towering height and took a slow, full breath. Then deliberately he pushed his trunk into the middle of the floor and began packing it, with the quiet method which characterized all his personal arrangements. At first, he worked in grim silence; then, by almost imperceptible degrees, his face lighted and he fell to humming over to himself the familiar song,--

"Even bravest heart may swell In the moment of farewell--"

Little by little, the humming rose and filled the room, at first the one phrase repeated over and over again; then all at once, deep and resonant, Thayer's full voice came leaping out in the rich Italian words,--

"Là sul campo nel dì della pugna, Ah! si, Fra le file primiero saro."

The past was already the past. "Blithe as a knight in his bridal array," Thayer was echoing the call of his future destiny. Because he had won a single battle, there was no reason he should lay down his arms.

"Careless what fate may befall me, When Glory shall call me."

He sang it boldly, joyously. He was not forgetful, only hopeful. He would leave to the choice of fate the field in which his mastery should lie. Master he would be at any cost.

"Careless what fate may befall me, When Glory shall call me."

For the last time, that little room was echoing with his voice.

His own rooms in New York were echoing with the same song, when Bobby Dane entered them, the next Saturday night.

"Well, at least, you don't sound broken-hearted," he observed, as he took off his coat.

"The sight of you would go far to cure me, if I were," Thayer retorted. His words were light; but his face and his grip on Bobby's two hands contradicted his tone.

"Glad of it," Bobby said flatly. "But tell me about Beatrix. How did the poor girl stand it?"

"Like herself," Thayer answered. "It was enough to shake the nerves of the Winged Victory; but Mrs. Lorimer went through it like a heroine."

"It was D.T.?"

"Yes."

"It was better that you kept the secret," Bobby said thoughtfully, as he dropped into a chair by the piano. He sat silent for a moment while, bending forward, he idly picked out the first few notes of the cavatina on the lowest octave of the bass. Then he added, "I don't see how you managed it, Thayer; but it is a good deed done. Was there any trouble about the certificate?"

"No. It was heart failure, true enough, and there was no need to go into secondary causes."

"I am glad the doctor was a man of sense. If he had been a martinet, it would have been worse for us all. Of course, there is no telling how far people will accept the story; but we may as well try to act as if it were true." There was a pause. Then Bobby inquired, "Well, and now what are you going to do next?"

"*Valentine* in *Faust*," Thayer replied briefly.

"The deuce you are! When?"

"Next Wednesday."

Bobby's face fell.

"Oh, I wanted you, myself, for that day. Isn't it rather sudden?"

"So sudden that I didn't half realize it, till I found myself at rehearsal, this morning. It is to be announced in to-morrow's papers, I suppose. Not even Arlt knows it yet."

Bobby meditated for the space of several seconds.

"Thayer, I am delighted," he said then. "I was so afraid your stopping now might mean a permanent break-up in your work. Now you are going into your right field at last. You've been too large for oratorio; you fill altogether too much space, and crowd out the chorus. You need a whole stage to ramp around in. Moreover, if I have any idea what Gounod meant, he had your voice in mind, when he created the part. Go in, and you are sure to win; and not a soul in the city will be gladder of it than I."

Thayers face softened. His life, successful as it was, had been singularly barren of endearments, and Bobby's words touched him keenly. Heretofore, only Arlt had manifested any personal interest in his successes, and Arlt was a true German, chary of his words. Thayer held out his hand to Bobby.

"Thank you, Dane. I believe you," he said.

There was a short silence. Then Thayer added suddenly,--

"What did you want of me for Wednesday?"

Again Bobby's face clouded, and he laughed uneasily.

"Something you can't and must not do, Thayer. I oughtn't to have spoken of it."

"What was it?" Then a new idea crossed Thayer's mind. "Something about Lorimer?"

"Yes, I may as well tell you. We have been telephoning back and forth, all day. They'll be down, Monday night, and the funeral is to be on Wednesday afternoon. Beatrix is leaving all the plans to my uncle; and my aunt, who is a sentimental soul and has no idea of the real state of the case, is insisting that the poor old chap shall be buried with all manner of social honors. It is to be a real function, and she thought it would be the most suitable thing in the world, if you were to sing at the funeral. I knew you wouldn't enjoy doing it, all things considered; but I couldn't say so to my uncle. All in all, it is a relief to have this other affair knock it in the head."

To Bobby, the pause was scarcely perceptible. To Thayer, it sufficed to review the years between his meeting Lorimer in Göttingen and that last gray dawn in the cottage.

"But it doesn't," Thayer said then.

"You don't mean--?"

"I will sing. We rehearse in the morning, and I have nothing afterwards until evening. What time is the service?"

Bobby Dane's call left Thayer feeling once more at war with himself. Worn out with the long strain of watching over Lorimer, exhausted with the agony of that hour in the cottage, it had been a relief to him, now that his work was ended, to throw himself wholly into the preparations for *Faust*. The needed rehearsals and the inevitable details of costuming had been sufficient to occupy his tired mind completely, and he had held firmly to his resolve to forget the past two months. He had been able to accomplish this only by getting a strong grip upon his own mind and holding on tightly and steadily; but he had accomplished it. Bobby left him with it all to do over again. In spite of himself, Beatrix's desperate question for "the black, blank years," drowned the familiar words of his cavatina and set themselves in their place,--

"Even black, blank years shall pass."

Impatiently he shut the piano and, sitting down at his desk, began studying aloud the list of stage directions which outlined his acting; but, in the intervals of turning a page, he asked himself over and over again whether any other life could hold a grimmer contrast than the one confronting him, that coming Wednesday afternoon and evening.

Wednesday came at last. Thayer had left his card at the Lorimers' house, the day before; but he had felt no surprise that Beatrix had refused to see him. He caught no glimpse of her until the hour for the funeral, and he felt that it was better so. For the present, their lives must lie in different paths.

As Bobby had predicted, Sidney Lorimer's funeral was a function. Everything about it was above criticism, with the minor exception of the manner in which Lorimer had met his end. Society, black-clothed and sombre-faced, was present, partly from respect to the Danes, partly from a real liking for Lorimer as they had known him at first, partly from curiosity to see whether there were any foundation for the rumors which already were flying abroad. The rumors embraced everything from meningitis to suicide, everything except the truth. And meanwhile, the Lorimers' rooms were transformed into a species of flower show, and, in the midst of the flowers, Lorimer lay asleep, his cheek resting on his hand, his lips curving into the old winning smile they knew so well. For him, as for Thayer, the past was passed and done. For him, too, the future might still be full of promise. Thayer, as he stood beside the man who had been his old-time friend, admitted as much to himself, and all at once the intoning of the solemn ritual ceased to jar upon his ears. For Lorimer, as for himself, the fight was still on. The arena had changed; that was all. Perhaps in the new battle, Lorimer would arm himself with stronger weapons.

Then the intoning stopped, and some one made a signal to Thayer. Simply as a boy, and with a boyish tenderness, he sang the little hymn they had chosen for him. Each man and woman who listened, felt gentler and nobler for his song; but only Beatrix, shut decorously in the room upstairs, away from her dead, realized that, for the passing hour, Thayer had annulled the passion and the pain of those last weeks, and had gone back again to the old, pitiful, protecting love which for years had marked his attitude towards Lorimer.

From Lorimer's funeral, society went home to rest and gossip and exchange its sombre clothing for its most brilliant plumage. Nearly two years before, society had taken Cotton Mather Thayer to its bosom. Now it was making ready to burn much incense in his honor, and its first step in the process was to make his opening night of opera one of the most brilliant events of the winter. With this laudable end in view, the house was packed, and the women present had drawn heavily upon their reserve fund of brand-new gowns which they had been hoarding for the final gayeties of the season.

Thayer, with Arlt at his side, lingered idly in the wings, while the audience listened with ill-concealed impatience to the melodious bargaining between *Faust* and *Mephistopheles*. Then the attention quickened, as every bar of the Kermess chorus brought them nearer to the moment for *Valentine's* coming.

Charm in hand, he came at last, and the applause, caught up to the galleries and tossed back to the floor, echoed again and again through the great opera house. He accepted it quietly, almost indifferently, and stood waiting for the storm to die away, while his keen eyes, sweeping the house, recognized here and there among the jewelled, bare-shouldered women before him the faces of the black-gowned mourners to whom he had sung in the afternoon. The sight brought Beatrix to his mind. He wondered how she was passing the evening, whether, from under the benumbing effects of the blow she had suffered, she were still sending a thought, a hope for success in his direction. Unconsciously to himself, his pulses were tingling and throbbing with the music, and the throb and tingle brought back to him the memory of the pounding of his pulses, that morning in the cottage, only a week before. He had almost yielded to their sway; then he had rallied. He had gone through the shock of Lorimer's death, through the hasty discussion of arrangements which had followed, through the saying good-by, with a calmness that had steadied Beatrix and had been a surprise, even to himself. It was more--He roused himself abruptly to the consciousness that mechanically he had been going through the scene with

Wagner, and that the moment for his cavatina had come.

Instinctively he squared his shoulders and raised his eyes. As he did so, he caught sight of Bobby Dane, and the sight recalled to him the half-dismissed thought of Beatrix. During the one measure of introduction, Beatrix and *Marguerite*, the cottage and the Kermess went whirling together through Thayer's brain, turning and twisting, intermingling and separating again like the visions of delirium. For that one measure, his operatic fate was trembling in the balance. Then the artist triumphed. Steady and clear, yet burdened with infinite sadness, his voice rang out, filling the wide spaces of the great house, filling the smallest heart within it with its throbbing, passionate power.

"Yet the bravest heart may swell In the moment of farewell."

The house was rocking and ringing with applause, as the song died away; but Thayer heard it with unheeding ears. His old destiny had fulfilled itself. The chord which closed his cavatina had sealed his fame in opera; but his fame was to him as ashes in his mouth. With that same chord, he had wilfully bidden farewell, not to *Marguerite*, his sister, but to Beatrix, the wife of his friend, Sidney Lorimer. And, as the chord died away, with its death there also died his passionate love. Who could foretell what its resurrection would be? Or when? Or where?

CHAPTER TWENTY-TWO

"Otto, how does it feel to be a celebrity?" Miss Gannion asked abruptly, one afternoon in late May.

The young German smiled.

"How should I know?"

"From experience, of course. Your artistic probation appears to be over. Your winning the prize for the suite has settled it for all time, and now I am doing my best to readjust myself to the idea that my boy friend Otto is the new composer Arlt about whom the critics are waging inky war."

"What is the use?" he inquired, as he crossed the room and sat down at the piano.

"Because I really must begin to face the fact that you are destined to be one of the immortals, and treat you with proper respect." Her tone was full of lazy amusement and content. "Hereafter, I shall never dare tell you when your necktie is askew, and as for training you in the management of your cuffs!" She paused expressively, and they both laughed.

"It was a blow to me to find that reputation depends upon such things," Arlt said, after a thoughtful pause.

"Not reputation; success. The two things don't necessarily touch each other. One is a matter of brains, the other of fashion." Her accent was almost bitter. "You have deserved one; you are beginning to have the other thrust upon you. How does it make you feel?"

"As if I owed a great deal to you."

The girlish pink flush rose in Miss Gannion's cheeks.

"Thank you, dear boy. But really I have done nothing."

Arlt turned his back to the piano and, clasping his hands over his knees, spoke with simple gravity.

"Miss Gannion, here in America, I have had three good friends, Mr. Thayer, you, and Miss Van Osdel. Everybody knows what Mr. Thayer has done to help me; I am the only one who knows about you and Miss Van Osdel, and I know it better and better, the more I learn to understand your American ways. It was not always easy for a woman in society to accept as her friend a stranger musician without reputation and without social backing, to acknowledge him in public and to insist that her friends should acknowledge him. At first I took it as a matter of course. I know better now, and I know that you and Miss Van Osdel must have given up some things for the sake of helping me along."

Miss Gannion paused, before she answered.

"Otto," she said at length; "I am a lonely woman, and my life has been broader for knowing you. I mean that *you* in the plural, for there have been a good many of you. Some have been successful, some have not; a few have become famous, just as you are doing. Some of them have been sent to me; some have come of their own accord. We have been close friends for a while, and then they have gone on their ways. Every going has left its scar. I was a woman, sitting still in my place by the fire; they were marching with the procession, stopping only for a little while and then going on out of my sight. It has made me feel so futile. But, of them all, you are the only one who has suggested that the *vivandière* may be a useful element on the march. It was all I could do, and I did it. I am glad if it counted for anything."

"Everything in this world counts but cipher, naught, or zero," Bobby observed suddenly, as he came strolling into the room at Sally's side. "You aren't a cipher, Miss Gannion. They're either evanescent or tubby, according to whether you look at their moral or their physical proportions. You don't fit either measurement. Therefore you aren't a cipher. Therefore you count. How do, Arlt? No; don't get up from the piano. You owe me a sonata, at least, to pay for the stunning headlines I gave you, yesterday."

"Was that your work, Bobby?" Sally asked, while she shook hands with Arlt. "I thought it must have come from the bake-shop where they do all the other pi. Did you see it, Miss Gannion? It reminded me of *A was an Apple Pie: Arlt's Art Analyzed*. Properly, the second line should have been: *By Bobby Bunkum*; but I suppose his ideas ran low, when he reached that point."

"I say, Arlt," Bobby suggested; "why don't you write a series of articles on How to Get on in the World?"

"They would only take one line: Know Miss Gannion and Miss Van Osdel," Arlt retorted, with unwonted quickness.

Bobby shook his head.

"No go, Arlt. I've known them for years, known them intimately; and look at me! I haven't budged an inch in the upward march. The fact is, I have just budged downward. My new underling is a boy of seventy and afraid of a draught, so in common humanity I have had to make over to him my warm corner at the editorial board, and remove myself to the chilly places below the salt. To be sure, it gives me extra good purchase on the devil, as my present desk is just in his pathway to the Chief, and I can smite him as he goes by."

"Does he turn the other cheek?" Sally queried. "One lump, Miss Gannion. I am still keeping up my Lenten penance, for I acquired the taste for it, and I can't bring myself back to the old extravagant ways. Next Lent, probably I shall mortify the flesh by taking two lumps."

Bobby handed her the cup.

"The other cheek," he answered. "Which do you mean? He's all cheek, all over himself, and it offers itself, whichever way he turns. Have you seen Thayer lately, Arlt?"

"Yesterday afternoon. He came down to my room to rehearse the songs he is to sing, next Saturday."

"What is Saturday? You fellows are going ahead at such a rate that I can't keep track of you, unless I have an engagement book for your especial benefit."

"Bobby!" Sally expostulated. "Mr. Arlt's suite is to be played, Saturday, and Mr. Thayer is to be the soloist for the concert. You oughtn't to have forgotten that, especially when you asked me to go with you."

"Oh, yes; I do remember now," Bobby replied serenely. "I knew I had some duty on hand for Saturday, just when I wanted to run up to Englewood for a little golf. What makes you do music in pleasant weather, Arlt? It's mean to keep a fellow in-doors at this season."

"It is our last appearance," Arlt answered.

Bobby raised his brows in feigned terror.

"Nothing mortal, I hope."

"No. We are going abroad, early in June."

"Just the other fellow's luck! I wish I were a genius, to go frisking about Europe instead of inking my fingers at home."

Arlt shook his head.

"No frisking for us. We are going to study."

With characteristic promptitude, Bobby dragged out his hobby, mounted it and was off at a gallop.

"That's always the way with you musicians! You work till you are tired of it; then you go off and shirk, and call it studying. I used to think you were the elect of the earth. Now I doubt it."

"Have some more tea, Bobby," Miss Gannion suggested.

Bobby waved her aside.

"Am I a child, to be diverted with soothing drinks? Never! I must have my cry out, Miss Gannion. You and Sally can be talking about the last fashion in peignoirs, if you wish. I don't know what they are; but I did a scarehead about them for the Sunday fashion page, last week. The woman who generally sees to it had mumps, and I substituted. I thought I did it superbly: *Death to Décolleté: Peignoirs Popular for Suburban Suppers*. That was the way I did it, and I was sure she would be pleased; but she cut me dead on the stairs, the first day she convalesced enough to be out. Arlt, musicians are second-rate beings, at best."

"I am sorry. Perhaps you can suggest a remedy," Arlt replied literally.

"Cast off your leading strings, and work out your own theories to suit yourselves," Bobby answered unhesitatingly. "Now look here, I used to think that it was greater to create music than to evolve literature; now I know more, I know it isn't. When a man writes a book, he goes ahead and does it according to the light of nature and the sense that is in him. Sometimes it is good; mostly it isn't, but at least he has done it out of himself and by himself. When you write a symphony, you do it out of yourself, but not by yourself. You do it by the exact rules that somebody else before you has laid down. You can have just so many themes and so many episodes, though it would puzzle the *Concertmeister* of the heavenly choir to tell where the themes leave off and the episodes begin. You know you have got those rules to hang on to, and they are a great support in seasons of mental famine. Two themes and a subsidiary, and a lot of episodes for padding: that's all you need, and they are bound to come on in just a given order. Can you imagine a novelist sitting down and fitting his work neatly into a box measured off into compartments: one hero, one heroine, one extra, plus episodic sunsets and moonbeams galore? Not much! He makes his rules as he goes along. Sally, which is greater, to create a gown, or to cut it out by a paper pattern?"

"To cut it out, of course," Sally answered unexpectedly. "The patterns never fit, and it is more work to bring them into the shape of any human being than it is to start out with a free hand, in the first place."

But Miss Gannion challenged her.

"Sally, did you ever make a gown?"

"Never; but that doesn't prevent my having theories," Sally replied airily.

"And I have had practice. I attempted once, when my years were less and my zeal more, to clothe an orphan with the work of my own hands. I thought I would operate free hand, as you call it, and I wish you could have beheld the result. The orphan's own mother would never have recognized her babe in the midst of the strange, polyangular bundle of cloth. I suspect that the same might be said of a good many novelists, and that a judicious trimming of the seams according to some established pattern might improve their work."

Arlt nodded approvingly.

"As usual, Miss Gannion has spoken wisely," he remarked.

"Miss Gannion has only echoed my words," Sally objected.

"Not at all. You said it was harder to work from a pattern; I merely suggested that the results were more satisfactory."

"Well, never mind," Sally returned promptly. "I don't care about that, so long as the vote goes against Bobby."

"And then, this matter of studying," Bobby went on, disdaining her interruption. "Now, when you get hard up for ideas, Arlt, when you actually can't get enough out of your gray matter to fill up your pattern, you go off somewhere and study something. Now, if I--"

"What have you to do with it, Bobby?" Miss Gannion queried.

"I represent literature, of course, just as Arlt represents music. If I were to go off and study something, what would you all think?"

"That it was the best possible thing you could possibly do," Sally retorted.

Bobby frowned.

"You are so feminine and subjective, Sally. I suppose you can't help it, though. But really--Arlt, for instance, has produced a prize composition, while he is still studying. That's exactly what we used to do in prep. school. Fancy a school for novelists, with night classes for indigent poets! It would be a parallel case; but what would be the effect upon literature?"

Arlt rose deliberately and crossed the room to the empty chair at Miss Gannion's side.

"All in all," he answered quietly; "from my slight knowledge of the teeming millions who are standing in line before the portals of American literature, I think the establishment of such a school ought to be the first duty of a self-respecting American government."

Thayer, meanwhile, was preparing for a longer absence from America than even Arlt was aware. The late winter and early spring had been for him a season of perfect professional success. *Faust* had been the first of many operas, for the illness of the regular baritone had taken a sudden turn for the worse and had ended his work for the season, and the manager had insisted that Thayer should fill his place. The event had fully justified the prediction of the old *maestro*, and in his operatic rôles Thayer was finding out where his real greatness lay. His mental personality, as well as his huge figure, demanded room to manifest itself. His acting was dramatic, yet full of control and reserve power, and his voice, fresh from its weeks of rest, richer and stronger than ever, was endowed with a new note of pathos, of longing for something quite beyond his power of attainment. Measured by the eye, Thayer held the world in the hollow of his hand. The ear alone betrayed the fact that he found the world as hollow as the curve of his encircling fingers. But when Thayer squared his jaw and threw back his shoulders before one of his great arias, eye and ear united in saying that the time would come when, by sheer might of his will, he would fill up that world until the weight of its fulness should fit his encircling hand with a contact as absolute as it would be lasting. Meanwhile, he was biding his time.

Nominally, he was going to Germany for a little study and much rest. In reality, he was considering an invitation to sing at Bayreuth, that summer; and among his papers was an unsigned contract which would keep him in European cities during the whole of the following winter. He was leaving his plans undecided, until he could hear definite news from Beatrix.

Living within a block of her house, he had nevertheless seen her but once since Lorimer's death. Once only, less than a week after the funeral, she had received him when he called. The call had been an uncomfortable one for them both. Neither had been able to forget that morning together in the cottage. It had been impossible for them to meet as if that hour had never been; neither could they accept the truth which had revealed itself at that time, and face its consequences. As yet, the time for that had not come. Nevertheless, they both felt relieved when the call was ended. Living side by side in the same social circle, they could not fail to meet, as time went on and Beatrix resumed her old place in the world. Any change in their attitude to each other would not pass unchallenged. They were bound to meet; it was imperative that they should meet in precisely the old way. They both were wise enough to feel that the sooner they met, the better. Unbroken ice thickens most quickly. However, when Thayer, after a half-hour of platitudes, went down the steps, Beatrix, locked into her own room, paced the floor, to and fro, to and fro again, like a caged panther, while Thayer walked the streets until time to dress for the stage, and then sang the part of *Valentine* with a furious madness of despair which merely added another stiff little leaf to his garland of fame. The next day, the papers waxed enthusiastic over Thayer's temperament, and Beatrix, alone in her room, read the papers and smiled sadly to herself as she read. Thayer's fate was, in a sense, less hard to bear than her own. He could find outlet for his sorrow. She, perforce, was dumb.

Since that day, Thayer had caught no glimpse of Beatrix. She had seen him repeatedly, however, when she had been driving; and once, at Bobby's urgent pleading, hidden from view in the back of a box, she had heard him sing *Valentine*. On the way home, she had decided that, after all, perhaps his fate was no easier than hers to bear. His sorrow had measured itself by the greatness of his personality.

As the May days passed by, rumors reached the ears of Thayer that all was not well with Beatrix. In her strict retirement, he could get no word from her; but at length, as the rumors increased, he sought out Bobby Dane. When he came away from Bobby, his face was stern and seamed with deep lines around his rigid lips, and he vouchsafed to Arlt no reason for his sudden postponement of the date for their sailing.

"The first of July will bring us there in season," he explained briefly. "I find I can't leave New York until after the twentieth."

So, in the first fierce heat of early June, the days dragged slowly along. Day after day, Thayer sat long at his desk in the attitude of passive waiting. Now and then he read over his unsigned contracts, wondering, meanwhile, whether he would ever sign them. If Beatrix lived, he had determined to spend the next year abroad. In the other event--He shook his head.

Nothing then could make much difference in his future.

CHAPTER TWENTY-THREE

During the second week in June, Beatrix's baby was born, and for days afterward, the mother's life, so long in danger, now hung by a thread. Then the good old fibre of the Danes reasserted itself, and Beatrix came slowly upward from the verge of the River of Death. Bobby's face cleared itself of its shadows, Thayer signed his contracts and, the next week, he and Arlt finally sailed for Europe.

In the long days of her convalescence, Beatrix manifested an utter indifference to the tidings from the outer world. She lay by the hour, her baby on her arm, looking down at the fuzzy little head and the red little face whose indeterminate features were fast taking the stamp of those of their father. Strange to say, the fact caused Beatrix no repulsion. The fires of her being seemed to have burned themselves out, and even her feeling to Lorimer shared in her general apathy. In the weeks which had followed his death, she had made up her mind that the baby would be fashioned in his image; and she accepted the fact philosophically, as a part of her life from which there was no appeal.

From the first, the baby was a quiet child. Apparently he shared his mother's apathy towards all things, and he lay by the hour in a sluggish drowse, leaving his mother free to allow her thoughts to wander at will. They did wander, too. Lying there, passive, in her luxurious room, Beatrix's mind scaled the heights of heaven, sounded the depths of hell. The one had lain within her reach; but she had never known it until too late. The other had crossed her path in the past; it was opening before her future. Her baby boy, so plainly created in the physical likeness of his father, could not have failed to receive something of his moral nature. She quailed before the grim promise of the future and, drawing the blanket over her face, she tried to shut out the sight and the thought of her child. And, in the first weeks of her wedded life, she had so longed for the time when a baby head should cuddle into the curve of her arm! At the thought, she pulled the blanket away again impetuously and, of its own accord, her arm tightened around the little bundle of flannels. He was not entirely Lorimer's child; he was her own, her very own. He must have inherited something of the sturdy constitution, the steady nerves of the Danes. The stronger, better blood was bound to triumph; and she would work unceasingly to oust that other taint from his nature. He was her child; she loved him, and she would give her life to the training which should make him able to wipe out the stain upon his father's record.

July was burning the white asphalt streets, before Beatrix was strong enough to be moved to Monomoy. Bobby dropped in to see her, the afternoon before she left town.

"Funny little beggar!" he observed, as he sat down opposite Beatrix and gravely inspected the baby in her arms.

"What do you think of him?" Beatrix asked, while she smoothed down the wholly superfluous skirt and then, tilting the baby forward, straightened the frills on the back of his little yoke.

"Oh, he's not so bad as he might be," Bobby responded encouragingly, as he snapped his fingers in the face of the child who stared back at him impassively.

The mother's face flushed.

"What do you mean, Bobby?" she asked a little sharply.

Too late, Bobby saw his blunder. In his consternation, he blundered yet more.

"I had no idea he would be half so presentable a boy. Just the living image of Lorimer; isn't he?"

"You see it, too?"

Bobby was at a loss to interpret the sudden incisive note in her voice. No one had warned him that the baby's likeness to his father had been a forbidden subject, and he could not know that Beatrix, in brooding over the matter, had reached a point where she questioned whether the resemblance might not exist solely in her own imagination. Bobby's next words annulled that hope and confirmed her fears.

"He's as like him as two peas, cunning as he can be. There, boy, look at your Uncle Bobby!" Bobby bent forward and with his forefinger gently tilted the little face upward. "Lorimer's eyes to perfection," he observed. Then, as he met Beatrix's eyes, he suddenly understood their wild appeal. Dropping the baby's chin, he laid his hand on his cousin's shoulder. "I wouldn't worry about that, Beatrix," he added reassuringly. "He probably will take it out in looking, and, for his character, hark back to some remote Dane or other. Lorimer was a handsome fellow, and the baby might do worse than look like him. Otherwise, he may go off on a tangent. Suppose he should take after me, for instance!"

Bobby spoke cheerily, hoping that Beatrix's laugh would follow his words. Instead, she caught his hand with her disengaged one and pressed it fiercely to her cheek.

"Oh, Bobby, I wish he would!" she cried.

Bobby looked rather abashed. He and Beatrix had been intimate from their babyhood; yet neither one of them was prone to self-betrayal, and this was the most demonstrative scene which had ever taken place between the cousins. As a rule, they were too sure of each other to feel the need for expressions of affection. For a minute, Bobby patted Beatrix's cheek with clumsy gentleness. Then he returned to the baby.

"Come here, old man! Come to your Uncle Bobby!" he urged, holding out his hands invitingly. "Come along here." And before Beatrix could utter a word of protesting caution, the baby was lying in the hollow of Bobby's elbow and blinking up at his new nurse with round brown eyes.

Bobby stared down at him benignly.

"Feels cunning; doesn't he, Beatrix? He seems to fit into one's grip rather well. One can't help liking the little beggar. By the way, what's his name?"

"Sidney," Beatrix responded quietly.

"The deuce!" In his surprise, Bobby almost dropped the baby.

Beatrix answered his unspoken thought.

"Yes, I have decided that it is best. I must meet fate anyway, and I may as well do it boldly, with a direct challenge. The name won't make any difference to the baby, and it may help to make me more patient and forgiving."

Gently Bobby laid the baby back into Beatrix's arms. Then he rose.

"No," he said slowly; "it won't make any difference, and it gives the chance of bringing the name back to its old standing. You may take lots of comfort with the boy, Beatrix. I hope so with all my heart, for I know how you need it. Things have gone rather against you, these last months; but perhaps the bad times are all over now." At the door, he lingered and looked back. "If you need me at Monomoy, Beatrix, don't hesitate to send for me. Sometimes it is a comfort to have somebody of one's own generation within hail."

Six weeks later, she realized the truth of his words when Bobby came striding into the room, with the family doctor at his heels. For the past forty-eight hours, Beatrix had watched convulsion after convulsion rack the tiny frame, wear itself out and die away, only to be followed by another and yet another. Under this new sorrow, the grandparents had given way entirely. They were powerless to help, and Beatrix, pitying their misery which she knew was more than half for her sake, had sent them away from the room. For forty-eight hours, she and the nurse had kept an unbroken vigil; and Beatrix had held herself steady until she had caught sight of Bobby's strong, happy, pitiful face in the doorway.

When she came to herself once more, she was lying on the couch in the hall, with Bobby beside her and Bobby's protecting arm around her shoulders.

"It may not be so bad, dear," he was saying soothingly. "Schirmer will pull him through, if anybody can, and he says it isn't at all hopeless. Lots of youngsters have convulsions and come out of them, jolly as grigs."

Beatrix saw no need for telling him the new fear which had tortured her, during those endless hours of waiting after she had sent off her telegram. Instead, she took his sympathy as it was given, with loving optimism; but she nestled even more closely against her cousin's side, as if for the hour she gained strength from the touch of his protecting arm. It was her one spot of perfect restfulness.

Late that night, Bobby had a talk with the doctor. It left him glad that already he had spoken with encouragement to Beatrix. The next two days, he gave his time to her absolutely. Then his official summons came, and reluctantly he returned to his desk.

By the time Beatrix was in town again, she was ready to admit to herself that hopelessness might mean something worse than death. By the end of the winter, the *might* had ceased to be potential and had become actual. Since those August days at Monomoy, the convulsions had recurred at irregular intervals. The physical constitution of the Danes had refused to give way to them; the nervous instability of the Lorimers had yielded to them utterly. Unless some miracle intervened, the child must face a future of vigorous body and enfeebled brain; and Beatrix, as she watched him, told herself the melancholy truth that the day of miracles was irrevocably dead. It seemed to her that the years were stretching out before her in an empty, unending trail, that she must follow it alone, hand in hand with her child, bound forever to watch for the signs of an intellect which never, never should appear. And she was the one to blame. It was no less her own fault, because she had assumed the responsibility in arrogant ignoring of its true import.

One afternoon in late May found her sitting by the open window with the child in her arms, when Thayer was announced. She greeted him with something of her old cordiality. Then she rang for the nurse to take away the baby.

"When did you get home again?" she asked, when they were seated alone together.

"This morning. I landed at ten, and I came directly to you."

She ignored the eagerness of his tone.

"You have been wonderfully successful, I am told."

"Well enough. It was nothing wonderful, though."

"Bobby has kept me informed of your glories," she insisted, with a slight smile; "and Mr. Arlt has really enjoyed them as well as if they had been his own."

"That is characteristic of Arlt. His letters were noncommittal; but Bobby says he has had his own fair share of honors. I am glad, for he deserves them."

"Indeed he does," she assented heartily. "We all are so glad for him; and it is a delight to watch the odd, boyish modesty with which he accepts his own fame. He is the most unspoiled genius I have ever known."

There was a short silence. Thayer grew restless under it. He had not hurried his return, left his luncheon untasted and escaped from a dozen reporters, in order to sit and discuss Arlt with that black-gowned woman the tip of whose finger outweighed for him the clumsy honors of the earth. All the way over, he had paced the steamer's deck by the hour, planning what words he should say to Beatrix when at last they stood face to face, with only the long-buried dead between them. He had supposed that lie had learned his lesson by heart. Nevertheless, now that he was at last in her presence, his words fled from his mind. Beatrix broke the silence.

"You have seen Bobby, then?"

"He met me at the steamer."

She raised her eyes to his, half-appealingly, half-defiantly.

"And he told you--"

"He has told me everything," Thayer interrupted her. He rose restlessly, crossed the room to the mantel and examined a vase with unseeing eyes. Then, returning, he halted directly before her, straightened his shoulders and drew a deep, full breath. "Beatrix?" he said unsteadily.

She shrank from before the words she had been dreading for so long.

"Don't!" she begged him.

"But I must." His voice was steady now. "We both of us know the truth, and the time has come when we can acknowledge it. I have waited long, dear, long and patiently. For fifteen months, I have left you to yourself and to the past. Now it is time for the future. I have come home, Beatrix, to marry you at last."

Before the glad tenderness that thrilled in his tone, she sank back in her deep chair and buried her face in her hands. Thayer waited quietly, patiently. He had told his story; he could afford to wait for her answer, since he never doubted what it was to be. The silence between them lasted for moments. From upstairs in another part of the house, there came a fretful childish cry. Then the stillness dropped again. At length, Beatrix let her hands fall into her lap. There was an instant of utter listlessness; then quietly she rose and stood facing him, drawn to her full height. Her cheeks were white, her eyes unstained by any tears, her voice quite level.

"I am sorry," she said slowly; "but what you ask is impossible."

He started, as if struck with a lash.

"What do you mean?"

"That I cannot marry you."

He stared at her in amazement, while the color left his cheeks and then rushed again to his temples where the veins stood out like knotted cords. For the moment, he was angry, baffled by the shock of her unexpected answer. Then he mastered himself.

"Do you not love me any longer?" he asked.

"Any longer?" Her tone sought to express haughty disdain; but her eyes drooped before the fire in his own.

"Never mind the words," he said sharply. "In times like this, one can't stop to pick for rhetorical effects. It is enough that I love you with all the manhood there is in me, and that for months I have counted upon winning your love in return. And now--"

She interrupted him.

"And now you have found out your mistake," she said sadly.

"Yes." There was a long interval of silence, before he added, "And is this final?"

"It is." Her stiffened lips could scarcely form the words.

He turned to go away. All the alertness which had marked his coming had dropped away from him. He moved slowly and with drooping shoulders. Already his face had grown haggard underneath the bronzing of his sea voyage. Beatrix stood motionless, watching him, struggling to master herself, to hold herself firmly to her resolve which had been taking shape within her, during all that past winter and spring.

Halfway across the room, Thayer hesitated, turned and came back to her side.

"Beatrix," he said impetuously; "we may as well face this thing squarely. It won't be the first time. We didn't wreck the future then; we mustn't do it now. The cases are different, though. This time, the danger lies in half-truths. We must speak plainly."

She attempted to check him; but, for the once, she was powerless to stem the tide of his words, and he hurried on,--

"We loved each other. There is no disloyalty to Lorimer in admitting it now. He belonged to the past, and, in that past, you belonged to him. The past is over and ended now, and, for the future, we must belong to each other. It is for that that I am here."

She tried in vain to control her voice. Then she shook her head.

"What has come between us?" he demanded. "You did love me. Look up, Beatrix! Yes, your eyes tell the truth about it. You love me now; I am here to prove it, and to marry you in spite of yourself."

Gently she put away his arms and faced him.

"No. It is impossible."

He wavered before the finality of her tone.

"But you love me," he urged.

She was silent, and stood with her eyes fixed on the floor at his feet. Then, of a sudden, she raised her eyes to his, and Thayer was dazzled by the light that was shining in them.

"Yes," she answered, with a quiet dignity which he could not gainsay. "And that is the very reason that I will not marry you. I love you too well--so well that I can never allow you to become the father of Sidney Lorimer's child."

CHAPTER TWENTY-FOUR

"I believe my world is overcrowded," Sally said, one January afternoon, two years later.

"Arlt, why don't you take the hint?" Bobby asked languidly. "I am too comfortable to stir, and she evidently wishes to get rid of somebody."

"Possibly she means me; but I was the last to come, so I shall outstay you both," Miss Gannion said, laughing. "At least, Sally, your hospitality does you credit."

With leisurely fingers, Sally was opening her teaball; but Bobby interposed.

"I wouldn't make any tea for us, Sally. I know you are afraid it may not hold out for your crowded universe, and we three have been here often enough to have dispelled any illusions about the quality of your cups. Two are cracked, and one has a nick exactly in the spot where we drink. I suspect Arlt of having cut his wisdom teeth on it."

"Only women cut their wisdom teeth on a teacup," Miss Gannion observed. "But really, Sally, I would save my tea until the crowd shows itself."

Sally shook her head.

"You interrupted me in the midst of my thesis."

Bobby interrupted again.

"It is our only chance to get in a word. We have to insert its thin edge at a comma, or else keep still. You never have any conversational semicolons, to say nothing of periods."

"As I was saying," Sally repeated pertinaciously; "my world is overcrowded. I have so many acquaintances that I never get time to enjoy my friends."

"What about now?" Bobby queried. "Here are we, and here is time. Which is lacking: enjoyment, or friendship?"

"Oh, this is an interlude, and doesn't count. We shall just get into the midst of a little rational conversation, though, and two or three stupid people will come in and reduce us to talking about the weather."

"You might send out cards," Arlt suggested, with the hesitating accent which was so characteristic of him. "Why not announce that on Tuesdays you are at home to clever people and friends only?"

"Yes; but it is no subject for joking," Sally persisted. "Last Tuesday in all that storm, for the first time this winter, Mr. Thayer came to see me. I know how busy he is, and I was just preparing to make the most of his call, when Mrs. Stanley came swishing and creaking into the room, and she babbled about her servants and her lumbago until Mr. Thayer took his departure. I wanted to administer poison."

"Try an anodyne," Bobby advised her. "They say that stout people yield easily to their influence. By the way, why is it polite to call a woman stout, but rude in the extreme to dub her fat? That is one of the problems I have never been able to solve. I used the wrong word in regard to Mrs. Stanley, one night, and she overheard me. Since then, she hauls in her latch-string hand over hand, whenever I turn the corner."

"Do you mind, Bobby?" Sally inquired. "The two most peaceful years of my social life were the years immediately following the day I advised Mrs. Stanley not to attempt *Juliet* in public. Lately, I have wished that her memory were just a bit more retentive. Tell me, has anybody seen Beatrix, this week?"

"She was at Carnegie Hall, last night."

Arlt's face brightened.

"Really?"

"Yes, I coaxed her into going. You ought to feel honored, Arlt; it is the first music she has heard, this season."

"Hasn't she been to hear Mr. Thayer?"

"No; she hasn't heard him since his first season. I tell her she has no idea how he has developed, nor how much she is losing; but she seems to have lost her love for music."

"Poor, dear girl! I don't wonder," Sally said impetuously.

But Arlt interposed.

"Isn't there a certain comfort to be gained from it?" he asked. "I hoped--I had thought music was to inspire and help people, not to amuse them."

"It does in theory," Bobby returned; "only now and then it reminds one of things, and upsets the whole scheme of inspiration. But I was surprised that Beatrix went, last night."

"What did she say?" Arlt inquired, with a frankness which yet bore no taint of egotism.

"Not very much; but her face at the close of your *Andante* told the story. You touched her on the raw, Arlt; but you roused her pluck to bear it. I think she will send you a note, to-day."

"I wonder if you realize what an event for your friends this symphony was," Sally broke in.

Arlt smiled. With growing manhood, his gravity also had grown; but his slow little smile caused his face to light wonderfully. Denied all claim to beauty, there was a great charm in the simple, modest dignity with which he bore himself. He answered Sally's last words with an earnestness that became him well.

"Without my friends, my symphony would have been left unwritten."

"And it was a perfect success," Sally added.

"Success is never perfect," he returned a little sadly. "Its merit must lie in its incompleteness, for that just urges us on to something beyond. The success on which we rest, is no better than a failure. Some day, I shall begin my ideal symphony; but, by the time I have reached my final *Maestoso*, I shall have learned that my ideal has moved on again beyond my reach."

"In other words, a real genius is nothing but an artistic butter-fingers," Bobby commented irreverently. "Stop your German philosophizing, Arlt, and help us enjoy the present by playing your *Scherzo*. Thayer says it is by far the best thing you have ever done."

Obediently Arlt crossed to the piano. In his absorption in his symphony, he had by no means allowed his skill as a pianist to rust for want of use, and a little sigh of utter content went around the group, as they heard the dainty, clashing notes answer to the touch of his fingers. He was in the full rhythm of his *Scherzo*, playing, humming, or whistling, according to his whim and to the demands of the orchestral score, when Sally gave a sudden exclamation of warning.

"Behold the crowd! Here endeth the interlude! Enter Mrs. Lloyd Avalons!"

"What in thunder is that woman doing here, Sally?" Bobby demanded, as Arlt's fingers dropped from the keys in the very midst of a phrase.

Sally shrugged her shoulders with the petulant gesture of a naughty child.

"How in thunder should I know, Bobby? I wish you'd ask her."

"No use. She never takes a hint."

A sudden change came over the group, as Mrs. Lloyd Avalons tripped daintily into the room. Miss Gannion straightened herself in her chair and took refuge in her lorgnette; Arlt's artistic fire extinguished itself, and he once more became the taciturn young German, while Sally assumed certain of the characteristics of a frozen olive. Bobby, however, continued to smile upon the room with unabated serenity.

"What a delight to find you here!" Mrs. Lloyd Avalons exclaimed, as she took Sally's hand.

"Miss Van Osdel has unsuspected depths to her nature," Bobby observed gravely. "Long as I have known her, Mrs. Avalons, I assure you I have never succeeded in finding her out."

"Oh--yes. How like you that is, Mr. Dane! But I was including you all."

"Taking us all in?" Bobby queried.

"Taking us just as you find us," Sally added. "You also take tea, I think, Mrs. Avalons?"

"You'd better," Bobby urged, with inadvertent pointedness. "We were just saying that Miss Van Osdel brews wisdom mingled with her tea."

"Bobby!" Sally adjured him, in a horrified whisper; but Mrs. Lloyd Avalons had already turned to Arlt.

"I am so glad to meet you here, Mr. Arlt. All your friends, to-day, are eager to congratulate you on your wonderful symphony."

"Yes." Arlt's tone was scarcely ingratiating, as he stirred his tea violently.

"Yes, it was beautiful, so sweet and harmonious. Really, you are quite taking the city by storm. You must be very busy to do so much writing. Don't you get very tired?"

"Sometimes." Arlt emptied his cup at a gulp.

"Oh, you must! But it is worth tiring one's poor head, to achieve such splendid results. But don't you ever rest? All winter long, I have been hoping you would find time to drop in on me, some Thursday."

"Thank you." Arlt attacked his extra lump of sugar with his spoon. Eluding his touch, it flew across the room and landed at Bobby's feet. Stooping down, Bobby rescued it and gravely handed it back to Arlt.

"Try it again, old man," he said encouragingly. "You'll get the proper range in time."

But Mrs. Lloyd Avalons returned to the charge.

"Well, as long as you won't come to me, I must seize my chance here, if Miss Van Osdel will excuse me. We are getting up a concert for the benefit of the Allied Day Nurseries, Mr. Arlt. It is to be very select indeed, only artists of established reputation are to be invited to take part, and we shall keep the price of the tickets up high enough to shut out any undesirable people who might otherwise come. We are counting on you for two numbers."

"But I cannot play."

"In other words, Mrs. Avalons," Bobby remarked: "you'll have to discount Arlt."

"But we must have him," Mrs. Lloyd Avalons said, in real dismay. "We never thought of his refusing."

Arlt shook his head in grim silence.

Mrs. Lloyd Avalons took refuge in cajolery.

"Oh, but you must! We can't spare you, Mr. Arlt. If you don't care for the charity, you'll do it for me; won't you?"

Deliberately Arlt packed the sugar and the spoon into his cup, and set the cup down on the table. Then he turned to face Mrs. Lloyd Avalons squarely.

"On the contrary, that is the very reason I cannot do it, Mrs. Lloyd Avalons. When Miss Gannion introduced me to you as Mr. Thayer's accompanist and a pianist who needed engagements, you wished to refuse me a place on your programme. Now that others have been good enough to listen to me, you can make room for two numbers by me. I am very sorry; but I shall be unable to accept your invitation."

There was no underlying rancor in the slow, deliberate syllables; they were merely the statement of an indisputable fact. Most women would have accepted them in silence. Not so with Mrs. Lloyd Avalons.

"But you played for Miss Van Osdel, last week," she persisted.

Arlt rose to his feet.

"Yes, I played for Miss Van Osdel, last week, just as I hope to have the pleasure of playing for her many times more in the future. However, that is quite a different matter. Miss Van Osdel and I are very old friends, and it will always be one of my very greatest pleasures to be entirely at her service." He made a quaint little bow in Sally's direction, and his face lighted with the friendly, humorous smile she knew so well. Then he added, "And now I must bid you all a very good afternoon."

He bowed again and walked away, with his simple dignity unruffled to the last. Society might bless him, or society might ban. Nevertheless, it was by no means Arlt's intention to turn his art into a species of lap-dog, to come trotting in at society's call, and then be dismissed to the outer darkness again, so soon as the round of its tricks was accomplished. Egotism Arlt had not; but his independence shrank at no one of the corollaries of his creed of art.

Bobby lingered after the others had gone away.

"I say, Sally," he remarked at length, apparently apropos of nothing in particular; "how does it happen that you have never married me?"

[Illustration: "'I believe I might as well ask you now'"]

"Probably for the very excellent reason that you have never asked me," Sally responded frankly.

With his hands in his pockets, Bobby sauntered across to the sofa where she was sitting. There he stood contemplating her for a moment. Then he settled himself at her side.

"Well," he said slowly; "I believe I might as well ask you now."

CHAPTER TWENTY-FIVE

"I almost made a whole poem about you," Bobby said to Thayer, one night. Thayer laughed.

"How far did you get?"

"The last line."

"Then you actually did make one."

Bobby shook his head.

"Oh, no. I only made the next to the last line and the last. Then the inspiration gave out."

"What was it?" Thayer asked idly.

The mirth left Bobby's face, and he looked up at his companion almost defiantly.

"Forget the things we cannot, And face the things we must,"

he said slowly.

The dark red leaped up into Thayer's face, as he looked at Bobby keenly.

"How long have you known it?"

"Since the day I told you they had come home from abroad. You sang *St. Paul*, that night, you may remember, and afterwards I advised you to go into grand opera. A fellow with a voice like yours can't expect to have any secrets of his own." Bobby paused; then he added thoughtfully, "Life is bound to be a good deal of a bluff for us all."

Thayer walked on in silence for seven or eight blocks.

"What do you think about it?" he asked then.

"I think that I would almost delay my own wedding, for the sake of being your best man."

"And yet, she says it is impossible," Thayer said thoughtfully.

"When was that?"

"Two years ago, when I came home from Europe."

"Oh!" Bobby said slowly, as the light dawned upon him. "That was the blow that floored you, that summer; was it? I never knew. What was the trouble? The child?"

Thayer's assent was rather curt in its brevity. Bobby's blunt, kindly questions hurt him; yet, after all, there was a sort of comfort in the hurt. After two years of silence, it was a relief to be able to speak of his trouble. It had grown no more, no less with the passing months; it was just what it had been, at the close of that warm May afternoon.

"Do you know, I rather like Beatrix for the stand she has taken," Bobby said meditatively. "She has the sense to know that, if she married you and made you share the responsibility of that child, it would knock your singing higher than a kite."

Thayer interrupted him impatiently.

"How much does my singing amount to me in comparison with my love for Beatrix? I would cancel my engagements, to-morrow, if she would say the word."

"But, thank the Lord, she won't," Bobby replied placidly. "Don't be an ass, Thayer. It is a popular fiction that an artist is expected to give up his work for the sake of matrimony; but it's an immoral fable. The gods have endowed you with a voice, and you have no business to fling away the gift, when your keeping it can do so much good in the world. You owe something to humanity, and a lot more back to the gods who gave you the voice; you have no moral right to do anything that will hinder your paying that debt. Beatrix knows this. She knows what would be the inevitable effect of saddling you with the child, and she is right in her decision."

"Has she been talking the matter over with you?" Thayer asked, with sudden jealousy.

Bobby laughed scornfully.

"No need. I have eyes of my own, and I learned my *Barbara Celarent* in junior year."

Another block was passed in silence. Then Thayer asked,--

"Do you see Mrs. Lorimer often?"

"Every day or so. I drop in there when I can, for she's not going out much, and she needs to see more people."

"How is she?"

"I don't know how to tell you," Bobby answered, while a note of sadness crept into his voice. "She is giving her life to that child; and, unless you know the child, you can't imagine the wear and tear of such an existence. I don't know which would be worse, the watching for the intellect which never comes, or the waiting for the convulsions that do."

"What will be the end of it all?" Thayer broke out impetuously.

Bobby shook his head.

"God knows," he said drearily.

Bobby spoke truly, for already it seemed that the divine plan was made to take the imperfect little life back into its keeping. A sudden chill, a sudden cold, and then the grim word, pneumonia! For days, Beatrix and the nurse hung over the child, struggling almost against hope to conquer the disease. Then it was that Beatrix realized how truly she had loved her little son, how she would miss even the constant pain of his presence. He was her very own, the one being in the world who belonged absolutely to her; and she fought for his life with the fierceness of despair. Then, just as it seemed that she had triumphed and the child was out of danger, the same insidious foe which had ended Lorimer's life, attacked the life of his child.

Alone in the dusky room, Beatrix was sitting on the edge of the bed, her arm around the boy who had just snuggled down for the night. Drowsily his lids drooped; then he opened his eyes, met her eyes and struggled up to reach her face.

"Mamma, kiss!" he begged.

That was all. Weakened by disease, the heart had been powerless to bear the strain of the sudden motion, and the boy fell into his final sleep, cradled in his mother's arms.

That night, Thayer sang *The Flying Dutchman* in the same city where, four years before, he had sung *St. Paul*. He had not been there, during the intervening time; but his public had been faithful to his memory, and the little opera house was packed to its utmost limits to do honor to its former favorite, as well as to its one-night opera season. For some unaccountable reason, Thayer had liked the place. Both the house and the audience had pleased him, and it had been at his own request that the manager had put on *The Flying Dutchman*, for that night.

During the last few months, *The Dutchman* had become Thayer's favorite rôle. Even *Valentine* had palled upon him in time. Lingering deaths become monotonous. When one dies them, four or five times a week, he longs to hasten the course of events, to change the *Andante* to a *Prestissimo*. To Thayer's later mood, it seemed that, psychologically speaking, *Valentine* belonged to the ranks of the tenors. His riper manhood demanded something a little more robust.

Thayer never admitted to himself that his liking for *The Dutchman* came from the personal interpretation which he put upon the story. In some moods, he would have scoffed at the idea that there could be any connection between himself, the successful artist whose single surname on the bill boards could suffice to fill a house, and the wretched *Dutchman* whose one defiance hurled at fate had condemned him to life-long wandering over the face of the deep. Of course, he wandered, too; but it was by easy stages and by means of Pullmans. The parallelism failed utterly. Still, there was the possibility of ultimate salvation gained through the faithful love of a woman. Nevertheless, Thayer's analysis always brought him to the conclusion that he liked the opera because his death scene was consummated in the brief space of two measures.

Thayer was feeling uncommonly alert and content, that night, and, moreover, he liked his audience. Accordingly, he gave them of his best. Never had his voice been richer, never had it rung with more dramatic power than when, in his aria of the first act, he had ended his lament with the declaration of his inevitable release on the slow-coming Judgment Day. Then he stood waiting, a huge, lonely, brooding figure, square-shouldered, square-jawed, defiant of fate, while softly the chorus of sailors in the hold below echoed the closing phrase of his song.

Even into Thayer's experience, no such ovation had ever come before. At first, the audience sat breathless, as if stunned by the might of his tragedy. Then the applause came crashing down from the galleries, up from the floor, in from the boxes, focussing itself from all sides upon that single, lonely, dominant figure before it. And Cotton Mather Thayer, as he listened with a quiet, impassive face, felt his heart leaping and bounding within him. He knew, by an instinct which he had learned to trust completely, that in the years to come, he would never reach a greater height of artistic success than he had done just then. One such experience could justify many a year of halting indecision. Puritan to the core, he yet had proved true to his Slavonic birthright.

As he left the stage with *Senta* at the end of the second act, a messenger handed him a card.

"The gentleman is waiting," he added. "He said he must see you, and that he was in a hurry."

Thayer glanced at the card.

"Bring him to my dressing-room," he said.

He glanced up in surprise, as the door opened and Bobby Dane entered. He had expected to see Bobby, immaculate in evening clothes, come strolling lazily in to congratulate him, as he had so often done before when Thayer had sung in cities near New York. Instead, Bobby was still in morning dress, and his face and manner betokened some great excitement.

"I only heard your duet," he said abruptly; "but they are saying you have outdone yourself. Will it break up your part, if I tell you some news?"

Thayer paled suddenly.

"Is Beatrix--"

"No; but the boy died at six o'clock, this afternoon. I went to the house; but I found there was nothing I could do, so I caught the seven o'clock train and came up to tell you. Sure it won't upset your singing?"

Thayer shook his head impatiently.

"I've borne worse shocks, Dane, and gone on warbling as if nothing had happened. Did Beatrix send for me?"

"No. I only saw her for a minute. But I thought perhaps you would like to go to her at once. She may need you."

Thayer held out his hand.

"This is like you, Dane. Thank you," he said briefly, as his man came to warn him that *The Dutchman's* crew had begun their chorus.

Bobby followed him into the wings.

"There's a train down at two o'clock," he suggested. "Shall we take that?"

"The sooner, the better."

"I'll get the places, then, and meet you at the hotel afterwards." And Bobby departed, just as the strings and wind gave out their announcement of *The Dutchman's* presence.

In the years to come, Thayer never knew how he went through that final scene. It was the automatic obedience of an artistic nature to its years of careful training. He was conscious of hearing no note from the orchestra, no sound from his own lips. His whole being was centred in the thought that at last Beatrix was free; that, in her final freedom, they must face the ultimate crisis of their destinies. Would it be for weal, or for woe? His brain refused to give back answer to the question. And, meanwhile, the close-packed audience was thrilling with the passionate pain of his accepted doom.

The crash of the renewed applause aroused him from his absorption and, hand in hand with *Senta*, he emerged from his watery grave to bow his appreciation. But it was not enough. Even to his dressing-room, he was pursued by the cries of his name. Yielding reluctantly, he went out before the curtain once again. Then he hurried back, and began tearing off his costume with a feverish haste which took no account of the time before he could get a train back to New York.

As Thayer's cab turned into the familiar street and stopped at the door of the Lorimers' house, the gray dawn was breaking. Before its wan color, the street lamps turned to a sickly yellow, and the asphalt street stretched away between them like a long chalky ruler bordered with dots of luminous paint. Above him, the lights in the house glared out across the sombre dawn, and something in their steady, unsympathetic glow, in the gray dawn and in the yellowing lamps carried Thayer's mind far back to that other winter morning when he had hurried through the storm to be with Beatrix in her hour of need.

The old butler opened the door to him, and took his coat. Then he pointed towards the library.

"She is there," he said softly, with an odd little quaver in his thin old voice. "I think you may go to her."

Thayer crossed the hall, laid his hand on the door, then hesitated. For an instant, he shrank from the scene that might be before him. Then instinctively he drew himself up and pushed open the door.

"Beatrix?" he said.

The color rushed to her face, as she sprang up and held out her hands.

"Thank God, you have come!"

THE END

* * * * *